"Travis Scholl contributes a thorough model for those of us who have little experience with the discipline of walking a labyrinth. Basing his multifarious reflections on the solid foundation of Mark's Gospel, he demonstrates the copious kinds of meditation latent in the discipline. This is a heart-provoking book!"
Marva J. Dawn, author of *Keeping the Sabbath Wholly*

"Travis Scholl has begun what I would call an efficacious recovery, bringing his whole person—body, soul and spirit—to the task. He also has begun to recover, for himself and for his reader, a taste for endlessness, a taste for the infinite. Presumably, most Christians once shared this apprehension of our being called into endless life, called into a faith that cannot be pared—without incalculable, disfiguring loss—into neat and conclusive propositions. Presumably, most Christians once knew that faith was not an idea. Walking the labyrinth with our hearts in prayer becomes, then, a way of our recovering a provisional glimpse of the Way himself, his inexhaustible love, his exceedingly great joy in our following him, now and ever."
Scott Cairns, author of *Endless Life: Poems of the Mystics*

"As Travis Scholl invites readers to join him in walking the labyrinth, he guides them not only along a spiraling path on the ground but also on a journey into the heart of Christian faith. Read and walk with him through these pages and discover new paths into Scripture and prayer."
Dorothy C. Bass, author of *Practicing our Faith*

WALKING THE LABYRINTH

A Place to Pray and Seek God

TRAVIS SCHOLL

Foreword by WALTER WANGERIN JR.

IVP Books

An imprint of InterVarsity Press

Downers Grove, Illinois

InterVarsity Press
P.O. Box 1400, Downers Grove, IL 60515-1426
World Wide Web: www.ivpress.com
Email: email@ivpress.com

InterVarsity Press® is the book-publishing division of InterVarsity Christian Fellowship/USA®, a movement of students and faculty active on campus at hundreds of universities, colleges and schools of nursing in the United States of America, and a member movement of the International Fellowship of Evangelical Students. For information about local and regional activities, visit intervarsity.org.

While all stories in this book are true, some names and identifying information in this book have been changed to protect the privacy of the individuals involved.

Labyrinth photo on p. 16: Dan Gill

Cover design: Cindy Kiple
Interior design: Beth McGill

Images: maze landscape: © James Thew/Fotolia.com
old paper background: © Kontrec/iStockphoto

ISBN 978-0-8308-3583-6 (print)
ISBN 978-0-8308-9593-9 (digital)

Printed in the United States of America ♾

As a member of the Green Press Initiative, InterVarsity Press is committed to protecting the environment and to the responsible use of natural resources. To learn more, visit greenpressinitiative.org.

Library of Congress Cataloging-in-Publication Data

Scholl, Travis, 1974-
Walking the labyrinth : a place to pray and seek God / Travis Scholl.
pages cm. — (IVP books)
Includes bibliographical references and index.
ISBN 978-0-8308-3583-6 (pbk. : alk. paper)
1. Labyrinths--Religious aspects—Christianity. 2. Spiritual life—Christianity. 3. Bible. Mark—Criticism, interpretation, etc. I. Title.
BV4509.5.S363 2014
246—dc23

2014022823

P	18	17	16	15	14	13	12	11	10	9	8	7	6	5	4	3	2	1
Y	29	28	27	26	25	24	23	22	21	20	19	18	17	16	15	14		

For Jenny

If the labyrinth is life,
we walk it together.

I thought of a labyrinth of labyrinths, of one sinuous spreading labyrinth that would encompass the past and the future and in some way involve the stars.

Jorge Luis Borges
"The Garden of Forking Paths"

He was in the wilderness forty days.

Mark 1:13

CONTENTS

Foreword

TRAVIS SCHOLL WINDS HIS WALK through the one labyrinth and all the labyrinths in the company of St. Mark. I can't think of a better companion—except that you come too—nor a wiser choice.

We end in the infinities. We end where we began.

This is the pattern of Mark's Gospel. Let me explain. In the smack beginning of his ministry, "Jesus came to Galilee." I don't believe this is merely a historical choice. In fact I think Mark knew already that he would end the story with much the same words. The white-robed man sitting in the empty tomb tells the women: "He has been raised; he is not here. But go, tell his disciples and Peter that he is going ahead of you to Galilee; there you will see him, just as he told you."

Mark does not end, as do all the other Gospels, with a sense of completion: a final commission in Matthew, an ascension in Luke and John. In fact, given that promise that the disciples will meet him in Galilee (if we accept the scholars' conviction that the Gospel cuts off at 16:8), Mark seems to have no ending at all. We end where we began, in Galilee! Why? Because Mark does not believe the story *has* an end. Having finished one reading, he wants us to read the whole story again—but this time in the light of the resurrection! And again, Jesus will "walk ahead of them" to Jerusalem. Over and over and over.

Travis Scholl's labyrinth is exactly like that! A walk with Jesus to be taken over and over and over.

But each new walk changes his labyrinth a little from the last because he uses personal experience throughout. Scholl's varying moods, his fears, his sorrows, his delights, constantly make each round new.

And so it should be for you who will read his book.

Once you have finished reading of labyrinths heaped on labyrinths, read it again, only this time read it seeking your *own* experiences!

This is the way of all personal devotions.

Walt Wangerin Jr.

part one

Before the Beginning

On Ash Wednesday, in the year of our Lord 2011, I began walking the labyrinth.

I have been walking it ever since.

I came upon the labyrinth by accident. In 2008, my wife and I moved into our home in St. Louis, Missouri, returning to our hometown after living in Connecticut for a while. Getting to know the neighborhood, I was walking past a church near our house, First Presbyterian Church, which sits at the dead-end of Midland into Delmar Avenue. Glancing at the churchyard, I discerned thin circles of cobblestone brick enmeshed in the grass.

I walked closer and recognized its circular pattern. I had heard and read about labyrinths before. And ever since college, I had read and reread the Argentinian writer Jorge Luis Borges (1899–1986), the writer whose paradoxical fictions are labyrinths, like M. C. Escher sketching with words. Now I stood at the literal foot of its infinite path. Its open entrance invited me.

I began to walk.

After that first discovery, I would walk its path occasionally, as the mood struck. For all I know, I am this labyrinth's only pilgrim. I have never noticed anyone else walking it.

The labyrinth first intrigued me as a leisurely curiosity. But then came the questions: Why walk a labyrinth anyway? What am I supposed to do as I walk it?

Walking the labyrinth—any labyrinth—is a curious thing. The labyrinth is a distinctive kind of maze. Its purpose is singular, as is its path. Thus it isn't the kind of game we typically think of when envisioning a maze, hoping we make the right choices to reach the end.

As a matter of fact, a labyrinth does not have an end per se. It has a center. And as long as you follow the path, you will reach the center. Every time. So there is a kind of mindlessness to the labyrinth.

But I soon discovered a purpose in the mindlessness. The labyrinth, paradoxically, stirs up a new kind of mindfulness, an awareness of the path that opens its pilgrims into a deeper sense of their surroundings, the lifeworlds—home, neighborhood, work, family, friendships, ad infinitum—in which they find themselves.

In short, the path of the labyrinth is the process of discovery. Its path is process itself. I walk the labyrinth to discover anew the worlds I inhabit. I walk it to discover what I thought was previously undiscoverable, what I didn't even know was there. Which is why I can walk the same labyrinth—time and again—and still find the path new.

What started as leisure was now turning to discipline. And the path is always new, because, as a spiritual discipline, the labyrinth is a path of contemplation, reflection, prayer.

On the surface of it, it is a place for silence and for speaking into silence, for speaking to One unseen. But beneath the surface, walking the labyrinth is a profound discipline in listening, in active silence, in finding movement and rhythm in the stillnesses underneath and in between every day's noise. Walking the labyrinth is an exercise in finding the voice speaking in whispers underneath the whirlwind of sound.

And yet beneath the silence, the labyrinth tells a story, a history.

Here is its beginning: Daedalus, the ancient Greek father of architects, built the mythical first labyrinth, step by treacherous step. At its center sat confined the grotesque half-man, half-bull named Minotaur, for whom it was built as a prison. As the story is told, Daedalus built the prison-maze with such intricate cunning that he nearly trapped himself within its circuits.

It would be awhile later, as Ovid tells it in his *Metamorphoses*, that the warrior Theseus would be forced to brave the labyrinth to kill the Minotaur. To keep from losing his own way, Theseus held in his hand a clue of thread, its thin, lustrous strand falling behind him to mark the path. The end of the thread was held in the hand of a companion waiting at the entrance.

The clue of thread was held in the hand of the smitten Ariadne, her gift to Theseus. Upon slaying the monster, Theseus followed the thread back out of the maze—his way of entering also his way of exiting—to take Ariadne's hand in his and sweep her away to the island of Naxos.

Thus the beginning of the labyrinth, its mythology. From the Greek island of Crete, extending south and east into India, north into Europe, west into North America, it took a winding, worldwide path, ever bending, never a straight line, always in circles. As it moved into Christian Europe—particularly northern France: the medieval cathedral at Chartres still houses a labyrinthine masterpiece—it became a path of pilgrimage and prayer, a living symbol of the journey of faith in a sinful, broken world. The journey in the *wilderness*. To reach its center is to enter the holy city Jerusalem and the mystery of the Christ who is the center of faith.

Long forgotten, labyrinths have been rediscovered in recent decades. Partly spiritual discipline, partly mystical fascination, partly cultural zeitgeist, labyrinths have spiraled again around the globe. They have become their own cottage industry. You can search online locaters to find one near you. You can walk miles in gigantic labyrinths set in stone. You can draw them on paper. You can trace a labyrinth path in miniature with your finger in a plate of sand.

There are infinite ways to walk the labyrinth.

Such is the ancient, worldwide story of the labyrinth.

But how does the labyrinth become a personal story? How did it become *my* story?

The story of the labyrinth became my story by way of pilgrimage and prayer. Or, perhaps, I became part of its story. I pray its path. Its path makes of me a prayer.

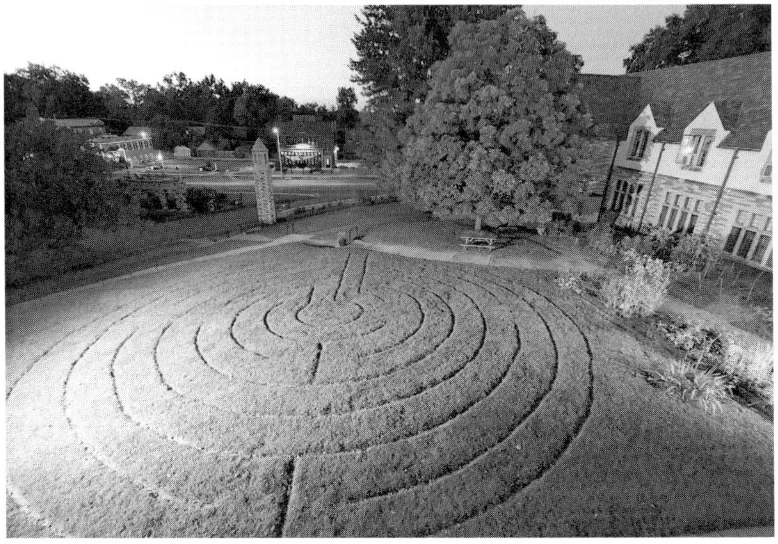

Figure 1

When we think of prayer, we think of words, of a conversation. Indeed prayer is this. But the labyrinth, as a discipline of prayer, is an *act* of prayer. In the labyrinth I pray by taking each next step, one foot in front of the other. The labyrinth makes of prayer an act, and it makes of action a prayer. In it, word and act are united, made one.

When I was little, this is how I was taught to pray: to close my eyes, bow my head, fold my hands. Then to speak into thin air. This is true. This is a way to pray. And yet the labyrinth is a physical reminder, a sign, that prayer is also a place, a space in which life—new life—is lived.

Prayer is not the thin air of a void.

Prayer is the world made out of the void, in word and action.

And isn't that what prayer is, after all, the making one of time and space, speaking and action, walk and talk, in the life of faith? After all is said and done, isn't prayer the uniting of one's life by listening to the voice of the One unseen, the One who kills and makes alive by one spoken word?

Oddly enough, this makes the labyrinth—the place of solitude—a place of encounter.

I walk the labyrinth in solitude but never alone.

This is the mystery of the presence of Christ in the world. Christ sits at the right hand of God, to recall Martin Luther, because the right hand of God is the whole cosmos, this earth, everything within it.

The One unseen becomes the One seen in all creation.

This becomes its next paradox: the path of the labyrinth is a process of encounter. This is paradox, because it is a solitary journey. Nevertheless, it is a journey to the center of things, of life, of my own identity, perhaps even into all reality.

It is a journey into an encounter with God in Jesus Christ.

And if the right hand of God is the whole cosmos, then all of life can be a labyrinth.

And in that singular encounter with the One who sits at the center of all life and all reality, I walk into ever new discoveries of who I am and how I am to live in the worlds in which God has set me—home, neighborhood, work, family, ad infinitum. And I am transformed by the encounter.

But how does the labyrinth—these thin circles of brick in grass—do all these things?

More to the point: How can I walk the labyrinth as a path to all these discoveries? I know of only one way to answer the question. And the answer is even easier than it sounds.

By taking the first step.

And then taking it one step at a time.

The labyrinth is a symbol of the living of life, one step at a time, one day at a time. The path of the labyrinth is the passage of life.

Life is a labyrinth. The labyrinth is life.

There is this incredible clarity to walking the labyrinth. It does not require some secret knowledge, some skeleton key, some solution to a riddle. It requires only the willingness and the honesty to put one step in front of the other and to follow the course it takes.

And yet it is filled with secrets, unfolding like the passing of time.

Of course, I write in hindsight. None of this occurred to me that first day, taking those first steps. It started with curiosity. It continued in discovery. It ended in encounter.

But to reach this particular center, it took another particular discipline, one that was spiritual, personal, daily. I really don't recall exactly *how* I decided to use the labyrinth for this particular discipline, other than the fact that I live and move and have being in one of the particular strands of Christianity that has this yearly liturgical habit, starting in late winter or early spring, of calling its disciples to a peculiar discipline. And so it wasn't long after my first discovery of the labyrinth in my neighborhood that I decided to use it as a spiritual practice for this special time of spiritual discipline.

The time was Lent. The forty days from Ash Wednesday to Good Friday. Every single day of the forty days of Lent, I walked the labyrinth.

Lent itself is a process of discovery. Forty days into the wilderness of faith, to every day walk a path of pilgrimage and prayer. At the center of the pilgrimage would lie the holy city of Jerusalem and the mystery of the events that would lead an itinerant preacher from a town at the edge of the outskirts of civilization to be raised upon a tree of pain, a ransom for many.

And just as the labyrinth is a place of prayer, Lent is a time for prayer, for contemplation, repentance, renewal. During my Lent, I exercised this discipline every time I reached the center of the labyrinth by praying the prayer Jesus taught his disciples to pray. The Lord's Prayer. The Our Father.

In the process, the labyrinth taught me the prayer Jesus taught his disciples to pray.

Only one question remained: What would be my clue of thread from

Ariadne? What could trace the path so that my ways of entering and exiting would not leave me lost?

The idea of the labyrinth is eminently more than just a physical structure, brick laid out in sod, mosaic tiles set in stone. It is a profound idea of art, the way M. C. Escher draws an idea that turns and turns again upon itself, the way da Vinci or Picasso draws us ever deeper into an image. It is an undercurrent of literature, the way a story by Jorge Luis Borges or Flannery O'Connor leaves us transfixed, the way a poem startles us breathless.

The idea of the labyrinth is all these things and more. It is the sign and signature of the undercurrent surging underneath life, underneath the ground we tread, the unknown life coursing within life, under its skin.

The labyrinth signals the unknowable center of life, its mystery, unseen and unheard in the babble and hustle of our everyday existence. In this sense, we need the labyrinth. We need it to remind us of the sheer mystery of life, the profound exhilaration of a breath when we stop to breathe it, the miracle of being still enough to hear the beating of our own heart in the midst of a noise that borders on chaos.

If for no other reason, we need it because it reminds us of the emptiness that lies at the center of our being. Such a stark-naked self-portrait might be too hard to bear if not for the fact that we spend too much of our lives tangling our days into snarled knots that clot the life that would otherwise flow freely. And whether we feel the knot in the physical pang of pain in our chest or in the sleepless worry of our nights, what we are feeling is our innumerable denials, our rugged defiance, inevitably our self-deception, about what it means to live and move and have our being in this particular world and at this particular time and place.

We need the labyrinth to remind us that there is a path that untangles the knots, a way that threads through our snarled deceptions, a pilgrimage into the life within life, the life transcending life.

I believe this same life within life drove a disciple whom the Christian church has historically identified as a man named Mark to sit down and write the story of one life that coursed through life so freely as to astound us all. By doing so, he set into swirling motion the sacred story of a labyrinth beyond labyrinths. He disclosed the mystery within mysteries, that one life could be lived for all life, one death could die for all deaths, and one rising would shine eternity into the babble and hustle of our everyday existence.

There is much to captivate us in the Gospel According to Mark's telling of the story. Its stark perspective. Its breathless pace. Its peerless eye for the telling gesture and the minute detail. And on a day in late winter (or was it early spring?), in a holy accident almost as surprising as that first day in the Presbyterian churchyard, I slid a hymnal off my bookshelf and counted up the number of readings from Mark in its lectionary. Exactly forty. With one more reading left over for the day after Lent is done.

This was the gift from Ariadne's hand. And I was smitten. The Gospel of Mark would be the Lenten thread to guide my way in and out of this, my labyrinth. The Gospel of Mark would be my daily guide on the path to an encounter with God in Jesus of Nazareth.

To walk this path with Mark's Gospel shows us that the act of reading can itself be a walk into a labyrinth. Our eye follows the lines of text, one line twisting into the next, follows the twisting path of words, their logic and image, in the hope that we will reach a certain center, a destination planned, or unplanned, by its origin. Our reading is all the more labyrinthine when the text we are reading is held sacred, when it is *Scripture.*

And just as there are many different ways to walk the labyrinth, there are many ways to read a book. All in one sitting. All in a week. A page at a time. A chapter at a time. On a beach. Under the light of a nightstand. . . . There are any number of ways to read the labyrinth of a book, even this book. But you may want to read this book in this way, namely in the way I wrote it. You can read each day's reflections—both on the labyrinth walk and the reading from Mark—as part of a forty-day discipline. The short chapters are numbered with that intention. The numbered chapters are grouped into sections that correspond to the weeks of Lent. And each section begins with its own introduction, a kind of interlude to bring things back around to a new beginning.

Of course, if you're reading this as part of a Lenten discipline, it is helpful to remember that Lent begins on a Wednesday and does not include Sundays. The daily Scripture reading index in the back provides the readings that accompanied my journey, should you wish to follow the lectionary I followed. But this is only a suggestion. As I said, there are many ways to read a book.

As you read you will notice certain ways that I use language. Repetitions of words and phrases are intentional and will, I hope, help the language resonate in your heart and mind. I return to certain ideas again and again, not to restate the obvious but to swim deeper into their significance. This makes a certain kind of rhythm central to how the sentences and paragraphs weave together, to how the strands of the various stories weave together. Pay attention to these things, to the ways my story, the labyrinth's story and Mark's story are interposed upon one another. I tried to write every word in a way that would give voice to the deep mystery at the center of life, the labyrinth of our existence.

Imagine the movement of this book as that of a spiral, like the double helix of DNA. The structure of sections—each with its own introduction, each intertwining these various stories—itself suggests a kind of double helix. In a sense, with each successive walk of the labyrinth, I felt as if I were telling the same story forty different ways. And yet each way was different, and each turn around and around invariably pushed me forward. I was moving in a spiral.

I have structured and written the book in these ways because the overarching goal was to echo the act of walking the labyrinth. And just as the labyrinth never moves in a straight line, I ask you to suspend your belief in the need for a straight-line, linear direction through this book to reach a certain destination.

Because I pray you can trust me when I tell you that we will reach a destination. And it will be worth reaching. Perhaps, in a sense, that is the whole point of the labyrinth, to walk it in the hope that it will lead us to the center of our life even when we think we've lost it, or, worse, it seems there is no center at all. We seek it to lead us to a center that is, in so many ways, unknown and unknowable. This is its paradox and its mystery.

Which leads me to the question that begs to be asked. What is the center of your life? Have you found it? If you think you have, do you think that you've plumbed its depth, that it has taken root in the core of your being?

If I could provide you with an itinerary for the journey that is this book, if I could say in no uncertain terms what this book is about, this is it: to find the center of life. My life. Your life. Our life together. And the purpose of the labyrinth is to show us that even when we think we've found it, its meaning is immeasurably deep, inexhaustible.

What is the center of your life?

Of course, I can't answer that for you. Nor would I want to. But what I hope I can do is to provide you a way to, both metaphorically and literally, walk a way to an answer. That's exactly what I did, walking forty days in a labyrinth in a churchyard three blocks from my home. What I found was that the answers the labyrinth gives are never the be-all, end-all answers we might want. They are always an invitation to fathom ever further into life's center, immeasurably deep and inexhaustible, ever winding in and around itself, in repetitions and reverberations, to a rhythm all its own.

As the apostle Paul would write in his letter to the Philippians, perhaps this is what it means to *work out your own salvation with fear and trembling*.

This is the itinerary for the journey that is this book, as best as I can write it, right here, right now. I write it for a destination that I know is there even as I cannot say where it might lead. I write it exactly *because* I cannot say, right here, right now, where it might lead.

And that is exactly the point.

This book does not require you to go out in search of your own neighborhood labyrinth, although that would not be a bad thing to do. It does not require you to spend forty days in discipline, nor to read Mark along with it, although those wouldn't be bad things either.

Here is the clarity of the life in a labyrinth. It requires only a willingness and an honesty to put one foot in front of the other, and to be open to the convergence of your story with the story of another, One who already walked this path long before either of us took the first step.

Perhaps it is no surprise that the Ariadne's thread for any journey of faith is the story of the Scriptures. But the convergence of these two particular stories is particularly fitting, because if there is any sacred book that reads as a labyrinth might read, I am convinced it is the Gospel of Mark. Why else would Borges, the writer of labyrinths, title a short story after it ("The Gospel According to Mark," first published in English in the *New Yorker* in 1971)?

Jesus, in Mark, walks a serpentine path and speaks in twisting parables, always winding in circles, never a straight line. At the heart of his message lies a secret center—Mark's so-called messianic secret of the kingdom of God—shrouded in the smoke of mystery. And in Mark's way of telling the story, the gospel is filled with paradoxes and reversals, just as a labyrinth's path leads to the center by ever leading its pilgrims around and away from it.

Stylistically, one of the ways Mark does this is through a technique scholars call "intercalation." More affectionately, it is known as "the Markan sandwich." It is the way Mark interrupts the telling of one story by splicing within it a second story. In Hollywood they might call it a "flashback," but in Mark these intercalated stories do not simply reflect back to the past. They push the story forward into the future. This feature, unique to Mark, thus produces poignant and sometimes mystifying interruptions in the narrative. Some readers cite these interruptions as signs of an inferior artist. But these interruptions—these *ruptures*—between the narratives tell their own story. Their fault lines shiver with meaning. This is part of Mark's genius: in the fractures of the story—

in the absences they create—new meanings, new *presence*, can emerge.

Just as they do in the empty center of a labyrinth.

I have stolen Mark's technique. By splicing together the tellings of two stories—my forty-day pilgrimage in a neighborhood churchyard, the pilgrimage of a preacher from Nazareth winding his way to his final destiny—I hope new meaning can emerge in the ruptures in between the stories, in the white space between the winding lines on the page, in the story of your life, even as it is completely unknown to me.

Because I am convinced that to walk this path is to walk the path of life itself, the labyrinth of labyrinths spiraling from past to present to future, encompassing the stars. This is the path of curiosity. This is the path to discovery. This is the path into encounter. We read it one word at a time. We take it one step at a time.

I invite you to walk it with me.

Walk the labyrinth.

1

Entrance

I STAND AT THE ENTRANCE TO THE LABYRINTH. The ground before me mixes with sky, gray within gray. A day of dust and ash. I have no mirror to see it, but I know my brow still shows a swipe of ashen gray above my eyes. If I furrow my brow, I can feel it crusting my forehead.

I stand at the entrance. I am thinking about death in dust. *Create in me a clean heart.*

I take the first step in between the parallel lines of brick.

One step. This is the first step.

Renew a right spirit within me.

I crouch down low, one hand on my knee. The other hand touches earth. The ground is thawing, waterlogged, but still cold. Late winter. Early spring. The lawn is matted a dormant flax blond, spotted with patches of enduring green. The bricks, ruddy red and brown, marking the boundaries of the maze, are slicked wet. The day started with a warming sun, but the March wind—floored by low-lying clouds—has now sped the air with a chilling bite.

I stand.

Before me, the gray and pink stones of a sanctuary wall. Slender charcoal windows, no light from within. Behind me, the rhythmic zoom of a busy street. The trees are bare. I hear one bird singing—perhaps a robin—but I cannot spot it.

The story of the labyrinth begins with its geometry. At the heart of its ancient design, the seven-circuit Cretan labyrinth, is this simple aesthetic paradox: the labyrinth creates a circle out of a square. By connecting four equidistant dots at right angles to each other with intervals of circling lines, it transforms the square into a circle. Or rather, it integrates the geometries of the circle and the square—line and arc, angle and circumference—into a single compass of movement and direction.

These geometries have a mythic history. The circle signifies the heavens, the square, the earth. Their integration in the labyrinth opens our sight to an ancient vision of reality: flat land within the arcing heavens. Ground mixes with sky, gray upon gray.

The labyrinth is a globe of the cosmos, square in circle. To walk it is to tread the universe underfoot.

And God said, "Let there be a dome in the midst of the waters . . . and let the dry land appear." The geometry of square and circle, the act of creation: the labyrinth is their story.

I take now one step, the first step, the beginning of heaven and earth.

The first step into the Gospel According to Mark begins in much the same way (Mk 1:1-8). *The beginning of the good news of Jesus Christ, the Son of God.* The first sentence of the first words of the Gospel of Mark—believed to be the first Gospel written—begins famously as a fragment of a sentence, all subject and no verb. The sentence is incomplete. And its incompleteness paradoxically throws us forward.

In a sense, Mark begins by trying to make a circle out of a square.

We look for the verb, the arc of the story. I look for the verb that begins the arc of my life.

It takes us to the *wilderness*, beyond the borders of what we know: our knowledge, our comfort, our expectations. When we go there, we go to the place of our own unknowing, to what we don't know and to what will be undone of the knowledge we think we know.

The beginning of the good news of Jesus Christ, the Son of God. The story has begun, and we are in the crowd gathering to hear.

If we listen close enough, we hear the story for the first time, again.

This is the paradox of the story, after all. We have heard the story before. But we are hearing it as if for the first time. No, this *is* the first time. It must be. Because we never know for sure if it will end the same way again.

These are the first words of the first story ever told. *The beginning of the good news.* We are hearing it again for the first time.

This is why, long ago, I was the child who would ask his mother for the same story—again and again and again—to drift me off to sleep. This is why my own son will ask me this night for the same story—again—before bed. This is the story's *mystery*, and we are entering it again. This is its hope.

This is the first step.

I take one step. I kneel. I stand.

I stop after one step, the long-winding journey of the labyrinth still before me. The *wilderness* still stands before me.

For reasons I cannot explain and dare not understand, I turn. I exit. This first step, this first day, this will be all.

For all I think I know, this is only the beginning.

Where does my story begin? My first step into the labyrinth? This morning when I first stepped out the door of my home? The day I tunneled my mother's womb to the light of my first day? The first moment I was conceived in that same womb? The first day God first spoke creation into being?

The answer to all these questions: *yes.* This first day is the day I take the first step into the labyrinth of all these beginnings. The labyrinth joins all these beginnings together. This is the mystery of the labyrinth of life—its story—circling round its source. Every step a first step. Every day a first day.

Where does this story—my story, your story, our story—begin?

2

In the Middle of Things

THIS SECOND DAY, I FIT MY LABYRINTH WALK into my day after work, on my way home. Driving there, I turn right, toward my house, before arriving at the church on the left. I am driving on autopilot. I have to turn around to retrace the route to where I should have gone, back to the churchyard.

I arrive *in medias res,* "in the middle of things," in an in-between moment of the day, in between work and home. I walk the labyrinth with some speed but not carelessly. The day has been cloudy and cold. I move a pile of thin branches that blocks my way. Near the end, along an outer circuit, but before it turns to move me to the center, the path turns me to the west. And I see, beyond the outline of houses and trees, in a break of open space, the pale orange of sunlight near dusk. But the sun—*in medias res,* hanging in the moment between day and night—still hides. Above me the speeding clouds are breaking late the blue of sky.

With swift step, I take all the steps I did not take yesterday. I am drawn inexorably to the center, the vortex of the whirling maze. Nonetheless, the path weaves in and out, toward and away from its end. It is as if to get to the center one must weave in and out within a rushing crowd.

I wonder.

Who has walked this way before? Who has trod this path? Whose footsteps am I tracing? In the pale orange of dusk, I glimpse a glimmer of a story that has been ongoing, for a long time.

I enter, *in medias res*, a journey much longer than my own.

Time moves us so fast. But if prayer transcends time, their prayers still echo here, *in medias res*. I walk in their shadow. I breathe their words. Their exhaling breath mixes midair with mine.

I enter, *in medias res*, a journey much longer than my own.

To enter into the story Mark tells is to enter it *in medias res* (Mk 1:4-11). Beginning to read the Gospel of Mark is like stepping into a revolving door spinning fast. Everything is action, speed and urgency. We start, it seems, *in medias res*, in the middle of the story. It is already spinning and being spun.

Time moves us so fast.

In the middle of our *medias res*, the Nazarene comes. He arises from within the crowd. No angels to herald him. No gold or frankincense or myrrh at his calloused feet. He arises from *within*, as if he had been standing here—among us—this whole time. Jesus of Nazareth rises from among us, drawn like us to the vortex of the whirlwind.

In medias res. This *medias res*. My *medias res*.

Just as the rush of water overflows the dust of his brow, catching in glimmers the pale orange half-light of descending day, we see the beginning take shape, his body lit with water afire. He is the center. He is the vortex, labyrinthine water swirling round him.

As we lean in, we hear the voice. The voice is not for all to hear. The voice is conversation: parent to child. *You are my Son, the Beloved; with you I am well pleased*. Said in the second person. The voice does not address John, nor the crowd. No one else hears it.

Except us. We alone overhear the conversation. We breathe its words mixing midair with our breath. We alone hear the secret whisper echo in our ear.

We are eavesdropping, listening in on intimacy, the indwelling of One in the Other. The exchange is so filled with power it breaks open the sky. It tears the cosmos apart. The power is the potency of love, taking wing in the Spirit. Three-in-One has touched down to earth, and the earth can barely contain the encounter.

As water soaks the linen of his garment, the love of One permeates the Other. The words are not directed to us, but we hear the voice. The secret blessing of it overflows me, permeates me, as water soaks linen.

The blessing of it—this journey much larger than my own—enters into me *in medias res.*

As I retrace my way home, I listen for the voice, here, now. I am encircled by its silence, the story of it, its secret blessing.

3

Wilderness

THE MORNING IS CLEAR when I enter the labyrinth. But the sun has not yet warmed the day. I see the vapor of my breath billowing before my face. The ground is covered in frost. It chills my feet. In the places where the slanting light touches the surface of earth, the frost sparkles, then melts. The circle of the labyrinth is cut jagged by shadow, the outline of the church.

Walking, I cross into shadow, then back into light. Along the line where shadow meets light, the border glitters, a halo inscribing the sanctuary's reflection on the ground.

The church is being made holy by light.

I am no longer alone. One life accompanies my walk this day. It is a skittish squirrel skittering up a holly tree against the church. Amid the ground's only leaves, deep evergreen, the squirrel hides from my view. But I am certain he is eyeing me, wary, suspicious.

I walk the labyrinth accompanied by wild beasts.

Immediately. The Spirit *immediately* drives Jesus into the wilderness (Mk 1:9-15). And never have forty days sped faster in the history of stories. We are breathless to keep pace.

But one detail is striking, and it is peculiarly Mark's. Jesus' journey into wilderness is accompanied by other lives. The *wild beasts.* I can only assume they are more beastly than squirrels. Does Jesus wrestle the beasts as Samson beat the lion with a jawbone? Or does Jesus howl in solidarity, each to the other groaning the brokenness of creation?

Perhaps both.

Is Jesus simultaneously wrestling and blessing the wild wilderness, making it holy by the light of his presence, just like the angel with wild Jacob?

Inasmuch as the wilderness is wild, Jesus knows it is also the place of hope. Forty days he spends there, as Israel spent its forty years. It was in the wilderness that Israel went to see God, that Moses saw God face to face. It was in the wilderness that Elijah heard a whispering voice and was fed by wild ravens. Jesus is bringing the wilderness with him, its wild hope, its manna, its promise of new beginning. As he speaks, our trust is unleashed, made wild by good news.

In the wilderness is hope.

If we are without hope in the wilderness, we are without hope in every place.

Mark says that angels attend Jesus, his daily provision, manna in the wilderness. At the center of the labyrinth I pray the Lord's Prayer. *Give us this day our daily bread.* The prayer and the provision are one. The same.

The prayer itself is provision.

Prayer is daily bread, my daily bread.

As I exit, my shoes leave faint, wet footprints on the sidewalk. They will soon evaporate. The traces of me will disappear. I start the car and National Public Radio updates me on an earthquake and tsunami striking Japan.

The waves are reaching the shores of Hawaii.

The coast of California is on alert.

One more reminder that just as sunlight sparks the annihilation of ice, rising heat ignites violence, even in the nature, the life, that isn't human. And in violence, the wild wilderness lifts the veil on what we thought we had domesticated. Without balance, the wilderness always reclaims what had been its own.

I have walked the third of my forty days. Already I am overwhelmed. Already undone. This is my wilderness, the labyrinth of wilderness. If I am without hope here, I am without hope everywhere.

My footprints fade on the sunlit sidewalk.

Prayer is my daily bread.

4

Work

COME, *FOLLOW ME*. The morning is quiet, a whisper. This is its invitation.

It is Saturday. Because I am not going to or returning from work, today is the first day I walk—three blocks—to the churchyard. My day is completely free. It is midmorning. When I am standing in the sun and the air is still, the day is warm. In shadow, the day is cold. The ground is thawed, cool to the touch, a soft sponge against my footfall.

Today I walk with my wife and son. When my wife sees the labyrinth, she is surprised. She expected a high hedge of bushes to mark the maze, as in an English garden. Instead, it is brick planted into the soil, flush to the ground. She and my son depart and I begin to walk alone.

As I walk, it occurs to me that the implanted bricks allow me to see the whole of the path around me. Nothing hedges my sight. There is a transparency to this labyrinth. And this is its difference from what we assume about a maze.

On paper, the child draws the line in the puzzle to try to reach the end, making choices where the trail diverges in two. There are dead ends and false starts. Bad choices. This is the *multicursal* maze, a game of choice. It contains many courses of action, multiple paths, only one of which will reach the endpoint.

But in the labyrinth, there are no dead ends, no choices to be made. It is *unicursal*, one course of action, one path, even as the one path appears to contain many. As much as this particular kind of maze appears twisted and broken, the way is one. This is the paradoxical transparency of the labyrinth, and this is the source of its trust.

This is also its freedom.

Its freedom embodies the difference between freedom and choice. We often assume our freedom lies in the ability to choose. But the freedom of the labyrinth is the certain freedom of trust, the freedom to follow a path that will not betray our confidence. I can see the whole path before me. I can trust it to lead me to the center, even as the path takes me away from the center, back and forth, ebb and flow, circling me around its edge. I can trust it even as I cannot see exactly how the labyrinth will lead me to its destination.

This is the transparency of the labyrinth, the source of trust.

This is freedom: to be able to trust those whom I love and who love me, to be able to trust those with whom I work and play. Of course, my trusts can be betrayed. And I can betray them.

Which is why our human trusts must be rooted in a more primal trust. They must be able to trust an Other whose promises make him trustworthy. This is the source of faith, to trust in a path that will not betray our confidence. Perhaps this is why the first followers after Christ were called followers of the Way.

This is the path of Christ. I walk the way of Christ, the source of trust.

The church sits on a hill. From the sidewalk below, the labyrinth is unseen. It is etched into a slanted plateau of lawn that, beyond its outer rim, cascades down to the street, leaving it hidden. But because of its slant, the labyrinth treks me both uphill and down. Downhill, the momentum of my body pushes me forward. Uphill, the weight of my body pulls me back.

I can feel its transparency, pushing me forward, pulling me back.

I notice ruts and pits in the earth along the way, some of which I can smooth with the stomp of my feet. In other places, I find myself again picking up sticks in my path.

At the bottom of the hill, across the street, stands a general store and café. It is called Winslow's Home. Through the windows, I can see the café is open and busy. But the streetside tables and chairs remain in storage. It is still too cold to eat outside.

Come, follow me, Jesus says (Mk 1:14-20 NIV). The morning is quiet, a whisper. This is his invitation. He stands on the shore of the lake in Galilee. The fishermen look to where they have been, then ahead to where they might go. The transparent laps of the sea push them forward, pull them back.

Their falling nets thud the sandy shore.

Jesus is transforming their work.

Jesus is transforming work itself. And rest.

Hear the quietude along the lake in Galilee: the cadence of shallow waves slipping on sand, the dull rub of rope against the hull of a boat, the intermittent groan of hard work peppered with banter, distant laughter, humanity hard at work.

The work of God has begun. It begins in the spiral of time in between work and rest.

Come, follow me. The irony is that I read these words as a sabbath, a day of rest from work. It is the labyrinth's invitation too. I stand in its center, pocket Bible in hand, its blue faux leather pebbled and soft in my palm. The warm Saturday is bringing the neighborhood back to life. For the first time, I walk the labyrinth seeing people who can see me.

I am not alone.

I wonder if they wonder what I am doing, walking in circles at the top of a hill, on a path they cannot see. I can feel self-consciousness, a twinge of embarrassment, slowly well up within me.

As I did yesterday, I speak the Lord's Prayer at the labyrinth's center. *Thy will be done*. There is still work to be done.

On earth as it is in heaven. The work of God's heaven converging with earth.

It happens in the spiral we walk each day, each week, in between work and rest. It happens with the same spiral that marks the path of the labyrinth. To move forward, we turn back around to where we've been, and around again into the future.

Pushing forward, pulling back.

On the grounds of the church near the labyrinth stands a statue of a man made of wood. He is pieced together by innumerable shards and slats and boards that have weathered to the color of slate. It is the remnant of a larger artwork. When the new pastor arrived, the church temporarily gathered hundreds of ladders from throughout the community, ladders from homes and businesses, ladders from neighbors and friends, ladders from other communities and congregations. An artist made of them a massive, meandering sculpture. It gleamed in the sun and stood fast in the rain.

It signaled a new beginning.

But now they are gone. Only the work remains.

On the shoulder of the wooden man he carries the only ladder left. He too is working even as he is at rest, a custodian of the yard. I leave the sticks I have gathered along the path—its own artwork—at his feet.

At the bottom of the hill, in front of Winslow's Home, I rendezvous with my wife and son. We meet people along the way, greet them with a smile. My love and I talk about pleasant things, everyday things. We walk along life's spiral between work and rest, the labor of love.

This is my Galilee.

Still near the beginning of this journey, I sense a turning in my work. And my rest.

Thy will be done.

part two

Christ, the Path

I guess it wouldn't hurt to come back around to the question one more time: What is the center of your life?

I ask it again because it is all too easy as a Christian to say that the center of my life is Jesus. That is the quintessential Sunday school answer. "You can have all this world, but give me Jesus." It is much harder to be able to discern what that means for every facet of my life and being, what it means for "every morning when I rise." What would it mean for how I live every minute of this day, for what I do with every cent of my money, for how I treat my loved ones, my neighbors, my enemies, every time I meet them? What would it mean for how I work and rest?

What in my life would stay the same? What in my life would radically change?

Followers of Jesus Christ have spent every single day of the two thousand–some years since that first day along the shore of Lake Galilee trying to figure this out, trying to answer such questions. And they have each come up with their own answers. It is, as it were, the labyrinth of labyrinths of what it means to be a disciple, a follower, of Jesus Christ. The journey of it is immeasurably deep and inexhaustible. And so it would be rather presumptuous of us, honestly, to simply wrap a WWJD bracelet around our wrist and consider the mystery solved. We wouldn't have really answered the question. And we might not be asking the right question to begin with.

Which gets us back to the original question: What is the center of your life?

Before we can get to an answer, perhaps we should start with a simpler question.

What is the center of the labyrinth? What does it, as spiritual practice, represent?

It is a symbol of travel, of pilgrimage, of wandering. It is a symbol of the way life brings us from one day to another, each day bringing enough trouble—and joy—of its own. It is a symbol, literally, of life's labor (*labor* and *labyrinth* share the same etymological root), a symbol of the hard work that life exacts from us, sometimes with purpose, sometimes without. It is a symbol of all the ways life revolves around a center, the moon around the earth, the earth around the sun, my own life around whatever it is my heart most desires.

As Luther would say, whatever that is, that is your god.

The labyrinth is a symbol of finding direction in the midst of the ambiguity, a symbol of the trusting hope that the path is leading us to a place where we can stand still amid the mists of mystery.

This is the promise I hold and I trust as I enter its path. Because so much of life can seem to meander and wander in twists and circles. So much of our lives can unfold from one day to the next without purpose, without direction. Ambiguity in the midst of chaos.

Or, at least, so much of my life has unfolded that way. I spent eight years after college wandering my way, wrestling with a sense of vocation, of a calling, before I entered divinity school. And many years before that, all the way back to junior high, when talking out loud about something like a calling would not go over well in the hallways of adolescence. I spent many years looking for signs, asking the same questions over and over again, overthinking my way in and out and in again to what I felt God was calling me to. Eight years felt like forty. Eight years of everyday life was moving me into a full and fulfilling adulthood, but nonetheless left my mind meandering around and around, revolving around a center that eluded me, in a fog of uncertainty.

Life has this dizzy way of spinning us in circles.

This much too is true of the labyrinthine life: the outward life that seems so sharply focused can mask an inner life of hazy confusion, a mental miasma. I have often wondered if the fog ever fully lifts. I often wonder if the crux of it all is to find the deeper hope that sees *through* the fog, no matter how thick. I cling to the labyrinth's promise that purpose is found *in* the ambiguity, or maybe even *because of* the ambiguity, even in the face of a terrible doubt that we may be wandering around without a path, nor a center, at all.

After all, without the ambiguity, there would be no need for the purpose.

This is what the labyrinth represents, right now, to me.

I have walked it four days. And I will walk it again to see in and through the fog.

Fortunately, the labyrinth, and life for that matter, does not leave us alone to find our direction. If we are paying close attention, it does not simply unleash us to the whim of "finding ourselves," to some mystical search into the unknown that is only a more intricate form of navel-gazing. Because at the heart of the mysteries surrounding the labyrinth, like so many circuits around its center, stands this mystery. Perhaps we could even say it is the mystery of its mysteries. It is the mystery that stands at the center of its history and its art.

The mystery is this: from ancient times into the Middle Ages, people conceived and spoke of labyrinths that could contain many paths, all but one of which was a dead end (what we would now call a *maze*). They could also describe labyrinths that contained only one meandering path that seemed confusing but nonetheless always reached its destination.

But when it came time to draw any of these labyrinths, to turn the descriptions of their structures into an image, they would only draw the *unicursal* labyrinth, the maze with the one path. It is only in relatively recent times that we have drawn diagrams of many-pathed mazes, the kind we find in children's magazines or the Sunday newspaper. We know of no visual representations from classical or medieval times of a multi-pathed, *multicursal* maze, even though the people of those times knew full well how to conceive of it. Related to this paradox is the historical reluctance of artists to depict labyrinths in three-dimensional structures, opting instead—almost universally—for diagrams, lines on paper. Even in descriptions of Daedalus's Cretan maze—a labyrinth of multiple paths so cunning it would take Ariadne's thread to escape it—any diagram of it is an image of a single path leading to a center, a pattern now known as the simple Cretan seven-circuit labyrinth. (The appendix to this book shows you how to draw one.)

Why would this be? What could explain it?

It is not because of an ancient lack of ingenuity or engineering. The ancients and medievals could build such cunning mazes. So they certainly had the capacity to diagram them. It would seem that they simply refused to depict them as art. Thus, the question remains: Why would they refuse?

The medieval church seems to have come to a convincing answer. As the labyrinth moved its way into Europe, and into many of the great churches and cathedrals being built there, the labyrinth's many kinds of paths were seemingly converted from a multicursal to a unicursal design. Every medieval church labyrinth is unicursal. This conversion was rooted in the same awareness that carried some of the classic moral labyrinths of the time, like Dante's in the *Divine Comedy*. This awareness mimics the dual elements of the labyrinth's paradox, that it embodies both wandering and purpose, chaos and craft. Dante can imagine, for example, a labyrinth of many paths that nonetheless, when one person successfully traverses it, maps a single path and pattern. This is the same thrilling awareness of the child who—finally—finds the correct path through the maze on the paper in front of her. The path of her pencil charts its single, snaking journey within the pattern of false paths. The faded lines she has erased from previous failures only reinforce this single true path.

The medieval church gave this awareness—both Dante's and the child's—a singular theological focus.

Jesus of Nazareth once entered into the labyrinth of life. He walked its path. He saw the footprints in the dust of all who had walked before (and would walk after) him, their dead ends and false starts, the confusion, the chaos, the misdirection. And in the midst of the ambiguity that seemed to cloud his feet like fog, he walked a singular path. He walked one path through the bewildering maze of bad choices and devilish temptations, the way through out-of-control circumstances and unintended consequences, the thin path between the rock and the hard place. He walked it the one way that could save life from death. He walked it the one way that could free our humanity from all that makes us inhumane.

This labyrinth charts his path.

And it will show us where it leads.

It whispers his invitation: *Come, follow me.*

The medieval-church labyrinth traced the path Christ walked on earth, giving it to its pilgrims as the way to walk the path of life, wherever it would lead them. In other words, the path of the labyrinth is Christ. Christ is the path. Walking the labyrinth—wherever it is, however you walk it—is walking the way of Christ, following his one path.

Of course, this is not to say that because Christ is the path there is only one way to walk it. As a matter of fact, the opposite is true. It is because he is the path that any one of us can find him in the singular walk that is our own life. Or rather, he finds us. *Come, follow me.* As many as there are followers of Christ there are ways to walk the path that is his life. This is the paradox, or at least another variation of it, that the one contains the many. Moreover, at any given point our lives open up several paths to us. Some of those paths will inevitably contain error, but often more than one of them will contain blessing. Christ, the path, opens all those paths to us with his blessing. I think this is at least part of what the apostle Paul means when he writes, "So in Christ we, though many, form one body" (Romans 12:5 NIV).

He is the one path that contains multitudes. He contains multitudes.

I walk this labyrinth to follow him, wherever he leads me.

Which is also why it makes such perfect sense for me to be reading one of the Gospels that give an account of his path to accompany my own. In a paradox akin to the labyrinth's paradox, the New Testament gives us four accounts of the path Christ walked on this earth, a multiplicity that shows forth the singularity of his life. I am reading the Gospel According to Mark to discover Christ, the path, hidden like a mosaic in the midst of my own, the path that he is making singularly my own. This path opens up the many paths of my life with blessing.

To walk these paths within a path will tend to leave us only with questions, two thousand years of questions, the same questions that will so quickly begin to swirl around the life of Jesus of Nazareth in the Gospel of Mark. The way of the labyrinth is the place for questions, even questions that seem to have no answers.

What is this? we may ask. What is this path? Why do I walk it? Where will it lead?

What is this? the people around Jesus asked (Mk 1:27).

Into the fog of our questions, he who contains multitudes will—finally—speak.

5

Threshold

W*HAT IS THIS?* The midnight and the morning have brought snow in the middle of March. A wet, dense blanket covers the ground. As I arrive at the churchyard, I stand at the threshold of the circle confounded. The labyrinth is hidden. The thin circles of brick make a depression in the snow. But it makes of the maze an impenetrable dartboard, concentric circles with no path.

So I stand for a moment and then I leave. I cannot walk the labyrinth blind.

I wonder: *What is this?* What is it that I hope to seek in this labyrinth? What does the labyrinth hold that I wish to find? What do I lose when it is withheld from me?

I wonder: What does the labyrinth hide? What am I seeking here?

Only this much I know: I seek.

As for the rest, I do not know.

I stand at the threshold of a path I cannot enter, and I do not know what I seek to find.

This day I leave more enduring impressions of my presence, footprints in the snow to and from the labyrinth. The snow is forecasted to become rain by nightfall. I stand amazed at the authority of the atmosphere in this late winter.

I hunger for spring. We have endured a treacherous winter, and I await the opening of earth to light and life. This will not be April's cruelty. It will be its generous welcome.

What is this? The little band of followers enters the synagogue (Mk 1:21-28). The man whom they follow is given the privilege to stand and speak. Keen eyes set in weathered faces turn to look. Ears leathered by the sun are cupped to hear.

The man speaks *as one having authority*. The congregation lights up with amazement.

This is the first day of the reign of God breaking into the wide world. It comes in Jesus of Nazareth, a man from a backwater town, encircled by backwater people. It comes with power. To, of all places, backwater Capernaum. The Nazarene has returned from the badlands—the wilderness—to enter the borderlands. With power, he arises from the farthest margins of power, among people unaccustomed to empowerment.

Thus their amazement.

They are the first witnesses of this new power of God unleashed, almost secretly, in the remotest parts of the world.

And just as much as we—the reader—have been privy to an encounter with Jesus to which the crowd at the Jordan was not, here the paradox is reversed. We are not privy to the speech of Jesus. His words are hidden, unrecorded, a secret. Only the people of Capernaum heard his words and their authority, a marvelous intimacy of words. They hear, and we watch what we cannot hear.

They are amazed, and we can only be amazed at their amazement.

What is this?

And it is here, now, that this man, his sinewy muscles still hot off the wilderness, performs his first act of power by driving out an *unclean spirit*. An exorcism: words releasing power against evil, liberation to the captive. This is *the Holy One of God*, baptized into his Father's love and driven by his Spirit's power. The vortex of his very being radiates with liberating power.

What is this? A new teaching—with authority! This is the first day of the new beginning of the reign of God. It rains upon the earth with amazed surprise, like a covering of snow in March. It comes in the life of the One standing in the synagogue and the circle gathering round him. He is himself a labyrinth of power. We enter his presence by the margins of the circle, the margins of our various geographies.

We stand at the threshold of a circle that seems impenetrable.

Like wildfire, the word spreads. And it will not be long before our question turns. *What is this?* will turn to deeper questions.

As I walk away from the impenetrable maze, contemplating a question from Mark, I remember that in house designs in ancient India, a labyrinth lay before the threshold. In solidarity with the myth of the Minotaur, the house labyrinth was a protection against evil. Whereas the Cretan labyrinth kept the monster in, the Indian labyrinth kept evil spirits out.

The underlying assumption was that evil spirits could move only in straight lines. Thus they could not navigate the twists and turns of a labyrinth. A labyrinth at the threshold was a lock on your door, a protection against the evils that flit seen and unseen in the air.

Evil cannot enter the sacred path of the labyrinth. To walk the labyrinth is to be exorcised of evil.

Likewise, in other places, a city was depicted at the center of a labyrinth. So often that by medieval times the drawing of a labyrinth simply became the symbol of a city. For the ancients, the symbol was Troy. For the Middle Ages, the symbol was Jericho. Like a winding city wall, the concentric circles of the labyrinth protected the community within from the evil without.

As one having authority, Jesus enters where I cannot. He walks the seven circuits into the impenetrable human heart. And evil spirits cannot twist to meet his power.

The petition of the prayer echoes in my mind.

Deliver us from evil.

The heart of Jesus of Nazareth is a labyrinth at the threshold of my own.

6

Worship

MY WORK TODAY MADE ME BREATHLESSLY BUSY, pulled in four directions at once. I do not return to the labyrinth until the end of day. Cutting along the boundary of our house, between blocks, a narrow walkway cuts through our neighborhood. I take it as a solitary walk to the busy street, which I cross to reach my destination.

I am exhausted.

A few clods of snow still speckle the way. The ground swells with water. I read from Mark at the foot of the circling maze, and then walk the way slowly, with intention. My arms are folded against my chest. I focus my gaze down on the ground before me. I sniff. The cold wind makes my nose run.

At the center, I pray. *Lead us not into temptation.*

A prayer prayed in tired solitude.

I close my eyes and feel how close I am to sleep. The gravity at the center is like a pole. It holds me upright and steady, and I am convinced I could fall to sleep right here, in the upright rest of solitude.

As I exit the labyrinth, it occurs to me that as much as the labyrinth weaves in and out from the center, it also moves back and forth around it. So I check to see if I can discern the logic of the maze. Back and forth through one quadrant, then around a semicircle and back halfway. But what I first discern as regularity is soon lost to asymmetry. The rhythm and logic of the pathway are syncopated, the step modified to its own beat. The movement makes of the labyrinth a slow pirouette of motion.

I am lost in the dance.

There is a kind of choreography to the labyrinth. Its history is part of the history of dance itself. As a matter of fact, some say that its original paths—where it broke and turned to wind and turn again—denoted the particular moves of the *labyrinthos,* the ritual, the dance. One doesn't walk the labyrinth so much as step to its cadence, the turns of its singular rhythm. But the particular movements of the ancient *labyrinthos* are unknown, lost to history.

On this tired day, I do not seek to recover its steps. I am comfortable enough just to walk it with my own.

The work has begun, so the day is long (Mk 1:29-39 NIV). The labor of God, the giving birth of the kingdom come near, has begun. This is perhaps the longest twenty-four hours in Galilee that Mark will record. But the day begins in hospitality. *Come, Lord Jesus,* we pray.

Come, Lord Jesus, be our guest,
and let these gifts to us be blest.

So goes the saying of grace as I grew up with it, before every meal. The grace we have in turn taught our child. Jesus is the guest at the house of those he has made his brothers, the house where they are also, in turn, children.

And yet, even here, work is to be done. We may not hear the man preach, but we see him act. And once again, we—sibling readers—return to our place as privileged guests in the story of Mark. Back toward the center of the labyrinth. We watch the solitary healer enter the room. Lamplight and shadow dance the walls.

We watch him take the mother's hand. He tends to her. The fever leaves by the tender touch of his hand, the soothing balm of his being. And one gets the sense that when he leaves the room—the woman springing to life before him—he is no longer a guest. He has made of this place a home again.

And he has become the host.

The labor of God begins in healing. Healing flows through him. As sunset culminates the sabbath of rest, the throng crowds the house made holy of God. Jesus, the newfound host, welcomes them. The labor of God is the work of healing, full and whole. And as the day is long, the night is longer. No one is turned away.

Who knows how long into the night he labors?

But by the end of it, his face is drained. He is spent.

His sleep is short. Before dawn, he leaves all behind, alone. He goes to the place where his spirit may be rekindled again. He strikes a solitary silhouette against the bloodshot sky. The work of the reign of God is invigorated by the energy of silence and prayer.

When the circle of companions—us included—find him, his face is flush again. He stands straight, his shoulders full and broad. *Let us go somewhere else.* As much as he is the host, he has no home. The labor of God is a homeless work, with a cadence all its own.

I am exhausted.

Jesus comes to his solitary place before dawn; I leave this solitary place at dusk. He starts in solitude. I end in it.

Does Jesus know something I do not?

Walking out of the labyrinth, drawing near the wall of the church, I notice a stone set into the soil. On it is painted one word: *Worship.*

Indeed, such silence is worship, a *labyrinthos* in syncopation with the Spirit. The labor of God has a cadence all its own. The busy street—Delmar Avenue—lies before me. To the west, it leads to the highway. To the east, the city's famous Delmar Loop, a hipster's paradise.

Let us go somewhere else. . . . That is why I have come, Jesus says (NIV).

Leaving the place, I see newborn color in the setting light. The bare trees along the street flush a bloodshot red.

7

Liminality

LUNCH HOUR. I WALK THE LABYRINTH TODAY in the noonday sun. The sun is warm. But its light, as well as the colors it enlightens around me, is pale and washed out. For the first time I do not wear an overcoat.

Every turn to the north, I see the stark lines of my shadow on the ground.

Where the sun hits land, it is drying out, as after the flood. Where shadows fall, the ground is still wet. I walk with my hands in my pants pockets, an afternoon stroll.

Across the street, the patio of Winslow's Home is filled with people. It is the rush of lunchtime. I find it difficult to look at them. As I make my circles, I look down for fear of their gaze. If they bother to notice me at all, I must be a strange sight to behold, turning round and round, taking the longest way round to reach the center of the lawn.

Jesus has gone on ahead, into Galilean country (Mk 1:40-45). He is on the way. His band of companions follow on his heels.

He is walking in the in-between land, from Capernaum to whatever no-name village will stop him next along the road. He is in the space of the in-between, the space between one place and another. He walks the middle passage, the land of liminality.

Strange word: *liminality*. Liminality is the time in between the first ring of the alarm clock, as we await the second. No longer sleeping, not yet awake. Liminality is the space of passing through, the road from one place to another. No-man's-land. No longer here, not yet there.

And there, in that lonely place, stands the leper.

He is the outcast. No, he is the outcast of outcasts. He is the down-and-out of the down-and-out. He stands at the city limits and at the border of taboo, unable to cross either. Others walk the long way around him to stay out of his path. Fear of contagion and death is an aura around him.

But, knowingly or not, Jesus enters this no-man's no-man's-land, and so the leper takes the only risk he has left.

If you choose, he says. The rumors of Jesus' power have reached even here.

And here and now, we are given the first glimpse into the inner life of this man from Nazareth. It spills forth in emotion, stirred deep and rending. Even as Jesus stops on the road, his heart keeps moving. Jesus sinks to kneel before the kneeling leper. They now meet face to face. *Moved with pity,* he crosses the ultimate border of healing. His arms stretch forth. And with both hands, he *touches* what is untouchable. His hands cup the leper's scaly cheeks. His fingers wrap round the nape of his neck. He lifts the leper's head until they see eye to eye. And slowly he pulls himself close until their temples brush, his mouth to the leper's ear.

He barely whispers into the withered ear. *I do choose.*

Only the leper can hear the words tickling his eardrum. *Be made clean.*

The final border has been crossed. *Immediately,* the leper can feel the flesh of his cheeks pulse and swell in the man's hands. He feels warm blood—new life—rush his head. He looks to his own hands, sees his body made whole. He is being made clean.

I do choose, Jesus says.

He chooses to touch with healing the outcast of outcasts. He chooses to lift the face of the leper.

Then spins the paradox again. *Say nothing to anyone.*

But the one cleansed cannot remain silent. This is the great secret of Mark. What the healer wishes to remain hidden cannot remain hidden.

This is the paradox of the secret, the secret of the paradox.

Why? We do not know. But from here on out, Jesus will defiantly and unwillingly enter the cult of celebrity. It will mean that this man and his circle will no longer walk freely, nor enter a place openly. The crowds will swarm. They will push against him and pressure them all. And the conflict will rise. From here on out, he will stay in *lonely places* (NIV), away from the welcome of a home. Rocks will pillow his head. Dust will be the blanket for his feet.

He has replaced the outcast. He has become the outcast of outcasts, standing at the city limits and the border of taboo. *Liminality.*

Here, in this lonely place, I stand. It is early spring, the liminal season. These are the days between the seasons, no longer winter but echoing its chill, not yet spring but hinting its warmth. *Liminality.* I feel the air touch my cheek, its whisper tickling my ear. Walking in the warmth, I can feel my cheeks swell. The blood flushes my face.

The path of the labyrinth is an exercise in liminality—the time in between times, the present moment that is both and simultaneously already and not yet. It is an exercise in how to still walk when the questions are as yet unanswered.

What are your unanswered questions? Do you still ask them?

The labyrinth holds their secrets in between the silence and the prayer.

Into this secret silence, I hear the breath of his words—*I do choose*—still stirring in stark light.

8

A Game

I WALK THE LABYRINTH TODAY with my two-and-a-half-year-old son. The sun-drenched day is unseasonably warm. As we arrive, I coax my boy to walk with me, to help solve what I have told him is "the puzzle." He takes my hand. As I walk the grassy path, he stomps on the bricks. I am lost in the play of his march. I guide him through the turns and listen to the clomp of his little feet against clay. He is bringing out the playfulness in the labyrinth. And in me.

When we reach the center, I pray the Lord's Prayer. My eyes are open to keep watch on him.

This is what I see in my prayer. My son continues to walk the circumference of bricks of the innermost circle, then finds in their border a straight line out of the maze. I marvel at the innate ingenuity of the act, finding a new way in what I had been wearing out. Sweetly he walks the churchyard. I follow his path to greet him again.

He seems to know something I cannot know.

He has made a game of the labyrinth. And he has made it fun to play.

Together we walk on to other places, the whole world the puzzle of a labyrinth before us.

One marvels at the innate ingenuity of four friends and the comic irony of the scene, a house made impenetrable with people (Mk 2:1-12). An immobile man finds a way through an immovable crowd to move into the presence of a man made immobile by the mass. The giggling starts quietly at the back of the room. The people there have the best sightline to see it unfold. The laughter echoes inward in concentric circles like the ripples from a stone thrown in water, only in reverse. It is only when the light spills upon the faces of those closest to Jesus that they look up and see what the back of the room has been watching all along. Dust falls in their eyes. Jesus puffs with laughter but keeps his lips closed, as if his diaphragm were sucking the laughter back in.

Then it all bursts out in a sustained bellow. Jesus roars in laughter.

The laughter stops when the mat touches the earth, and the paralytic lies at the center of the inner circle. The crowd makes room for the man but then sucks back in even closer. The whirlpool of people squeezes in to see.

Jesus looks up at the four friends—two men and two women—peering down. Jesus looks down into the paralytic's eyes. They are twitching back at him, the only part of his body that moves. A hushed moment feels like an hour.

Then the words.

Your sins are forgiven.

The eyes stop twitching and widen with awe. The sound of the words crackles electric. We hear the word now, the word spoken at Capernaum. We hear it for the first time. This is the word he is preaching. This is the beginning of good news. This is the new beginning of words themselves, as if all words now sound new. Not that this man's sins were the cause of his paralysis. But that this other man has the power to forgive what has weighed him down, what has paralyzed his soul.

With the words, he speaks with all the power of an unspeakable divinity.

Which is why the words cannot be spoken without conflict. We feel the conflict rise with the body's heat, flushing the face. Laughter has left the room. The authorities at the back of the room murmur into the vacuum.

Jesus' face turns tragically stern. He looks around. He speaks again, loudly.

Which is easier?

He answers their unspoken questions with a question of his own, out loud. The question is asked with such intensity that no one dares answer. No one knows the answer.

In the midst of his speaking, Jesus turns his face again, from his accusers to the one who can no longer be accused. In a moment the paralytic will rise, feebly but in full view. The four friends scurry back down to the front of the house to greet him as he weaves his way out of the labyrinth of people. As they glide away, their laughter fades into the distance.

Jesus, his taut figure awash under the spotlight of a noontime sun, now draws his face down toward the floor. No other crowded soul moves. Along the sandy floor before him, a thin line marks the shift of the sweeping sun, light from shadow.

In the distance, we still hear them. They giggle like children, playing a game in the sun.

As I walk and run and play with my child, the words of the prayer ring in my ears.

Forgive us our trespasses.

It is as if my own child lowered me into the center of this labyrinthine day, releasing me from paralysis. The good news of the words—forgiveness, freely given, freely received—is as astounding now as when first spoken. I laugh with the sound of the words, the way their good news liberates us to a childlike freedom.

If only it were always this easy, like a game children play.

Or maybe, just maybe, it is.

9

Rain

TODAY BRINGS BACK A CHILLING EDGE TO THE WEATHER. And as I arrive at the labyrinth at midday, it begins to rain. It pours the heavy, fat drops that make a ruckus on roofs and in trees. They bring with them the earthy, metallic smell of early spring. The water will bring to life what is still dormant, I know. But it keeps me from performing my discipline, my fast.

I have no umbrella. I am not wearing an overcoat. I will need to return to work dry.

Walking this labyrinth is the center of my daily Lenten fast. So quickly an inner righteous dilemma becomes my own. Should I risk a drenching for the sake of my discipline? How important is it to me?

If I skip once now, by the end my resolve will be gone, like a bad New Year's resolution.

But what if the end is now? What if this is the only day I have?

What is the line between discipline and recklessness? Between tradition and invention? How wide is the line of gray between the black and the white?

Levi sits in his customs booth, counting money (Mk 2:13-22). Nearly every dirty dime will go into hands more powerful than his. He knows that he trades in the crooked exchange of empire. He knows nothing is free. He knows the deals he makes make a profit for only one if they profit any at all.

All hail Caesar.

It is the reason he is hated by most. It is the reason he is bullied by the rest. It is the reason he is losing his hair. His belly burns. It is the reason he can do nothing more after the day is done than to sit at his kitchen table and stare. It is the reason his days feel like a perpetual hangover of cheap wine.

And it is the reason why when Jesus says *follow me,* he wastes no moment to get up, to leave everything old, to let it all go. One voice, filled with the sparkling light of the sea, was all he had to hear.

Immediately, a heart is changed, reborn.

And joy enters this life like a feast. So Levi can think of no better thing than to welcome Jesus and his new companions to his home. For a feast.

There is irony here. Only by calling to himself one who is hated—one who would never be welcomed in a righteous home—can Jesus be welcomed again into any home, to enter again into a former hospitality. No surprise that the hospitality too becomes hated.

If we are being honest, the righteous dilemma is undeniable. Jesus is crossing uncrossable lines. He says he has come for the oppressed, and yet he calls to himself a steward of the oppressor.

Thus the question: Is his reign for the powerful or the powerless?

Thus the paradox of the reign of God in Jesus of Nazareth. Everything—every single thing—in heaven, on earth, is being made new. The nature of power itself is being made new. The Son of Man comes not only to forgive sins but to call sinners into his inner circle. With forgiveness comes the calling. And he is ever willing to cross the borders between tradition and invention, discipline and recklessness, to make the invitation. The reign he brings into the world is not a bandage. It is a whole new medicine. It is not a patch but a new robe of whole cloth. It is not old wine but new. And it can be contained only in new skins.

To not eat at the table of sinners forgiven is to deny the forgiveness available to all.

As I sit in my car with my righteous dilemma, I recall the symbolism of the labyrinth. The labyrinth is a sign of both birth and rebirth. Leonardo da Vinci depicted the uterus as folded into seven cells, the anatomy of a labyrinth. In India and Native America, the drawing of the labyrinth was the symbol of the womb, the labyrinth of anatomy.

I am reminded of the way Luther talked about the *platzregen*, the passing rain shower, the way the good news, the reign of God, pours down from the skies, now in one place, then in another, all of its own accord, upon sinner and saint alike. The reign of God showers the earth with the birth and rebirth of all living things.

In medieval France, the labyrinth often took the shape of the octagon, the shape of the baptismal font, the eight-sided symbol of water and rebirth.

Again, Leonardo da Vinci drew designs of eight-sided labyrinthine rooms with walls of mirrors, presumably to allow the one standing in the center to see himself or herself from every side, infinitely.

Birth and rebirth: to walk the labyrinth is to be changed from one life to another, to see yourself from a center allowing infinite reflections, an utterly transparent self-awareness. The labyrinth is a sign of birth and rebirth. I read the Gospel of Mark in the cocoon—the womb—of my car, raindrops smacking metal into a roar. I see myself in the rearview mirror. I take a few deep breaths and let my shoulders relax. I see through myself and look through the windshield to see shapes distorted, abstracted, by rain. A wiggling tree. The smudging of a stone wall. A view of the world changed by the clear prism of water. A world transformed by a narrow passage through water.

Whatever it is I am seeking, I see myself seeking it.

I can see the reflection of my face in the pane of glass, an image reimagined, reborn, by drops of water. Whatever it is I am seeking, I see myself seeking it. My face is distorted by rain.

And there is a voice underneath the babble of the rain.

Follow me, it says.

This is not the end of the world.

It is the start of a new one.

I start the car. I let go. I move on, reborn.

Drowned out by the noise of feasting, a more threatening rain still gathers on the horizon. It is foreboded in the undercurrent of Jesus' words, spoken low. It is almost missed if we do not listen closely enough.

The days will come when the bridegroom is taken away.

In the house of Levi, amid reveling, it is almost as if Jesus speaks to no one but himself.

In the house of Levi, the revelers are oblivious. The time for feasting will be short.

The passing rain shower will pass once more.

10

The Signs

I WALK THE LABYRINTH TODAY CASUALLY. The day is cool. Light sifts through a mesh of clouds. Yesterday's rain has birthed new life. As I walk, I notice three fresh, small holes dug in different places along my way. Squirrels have been digging up the nuts they have stored for winter. They are doing what they know to do, filling their long winter hunger with good things.

As I walk, I remember the first time I walked the labyrinth, sometime before I started this discipline. The overgrown path wasn't always clear. Somewhere along the way I took a wrong turn. I never reached the center. As I backtracked, I saw that at one turn the bricks had been overrun by mud. I missed the turn. A few months later, I passed by again and saw that the congregation had cleaned and reshaped the maze. The path was again open and clear and free.

I stand at the center. It occurs to me that there are two ways of exiting the labyrinth once the center is reached. The one is to simply return the way I came, retracing my steps to the entrance. This has been my practice.

The other is simply to step over the boundaries and walk out. This second way may seem a violation of the path, but if the center is the goal, once the center is reached the path has performed its purpose. We are free to move on.

Or so it seems to me at this given moment.

One Sabbath. Some time has passed since Levi's feast (Mk 2:23–3:6 NIV). What has previously been a fluid account now becomes episodic, sporadic. Mark will flit here then there, marking new episodes—new rain showers—in the reign of God.

We are entering into the middle passage of the good news.

I have always imagined the disciples walking through this wheat field in a kind of slapstick cavalcade, casual and free. And the way they pop the wheat kernels off the stalks and lift the palms of their hands to their mouths is carefree, like cracking peanut shells at a baseball game. As they walk the land, they do what they know to do.

As they follow this new rabbi, this is their year of Jubilee. Their living echoes the jubilee life envisioned by Torah. This is the time of good news for the poor, healing for the brokenhearted, liberty for the captive, release for all in bondage.

The freedom he gives so freely makes it so.

As I retrace my steps out of the labyrinth, I come to an outer circuit where the outer rim of brick touches the concrete of the sidewalk. I stop. I take one step to the side, onto the sidewalk. I cross the border and step out of the labyrinth. Carefree. Casual and free.

Like the disciples. Like the squirrel.

But the labyrinth of my mind continues beyond the maze, beyond the churchyard.

On my walk home, I notice all the regulations that safeguard my navigation, that regulate all the possible interactions between streets, vehicles and pedestrians. I press the button on the stoplight to gain the right of way to cross the street. On my three-block walk home, I count all the signs along the way. I count no fewer than twelve different street signs, each one articulating its own rule for the road. Each avenue I cross in my neighborhood bears the same blue sign.

PRIVATE STREET

NO PUBLIC PARKING

STREET NOT THRU

Am I made for these laws? Are these laws made for me? The labyrinth too is a regulated way. Am I made for the labyrinth? Is the labyrinth made for me?

On the face of it, the answer seems simple.

But is there really more than one way out of the labyrinth? If I am free to arbitrate which lines I can cross and which I keep, where am I left? These laws are made for my safe passage. And there is indeed a part of me that is made by these laws, the laws by which I find a particular identity and a certain capacity to act. As much as they might seem to restrict what I do, there is also a part of them that empowers me to find the freedom within their form.

There is freedom in form. And the freedom outside form is a different freedom altogether.

Daedalus made the labyrinth. But the labyrinth is making me.

Which is lawful on the Sabbath? Jesus asks. The man with the withered hand stands before them all, his hand quivering. This is the alternative Jesus has set before the authorities around him. We know that Jesus has set his feet to cross borders. We know he has cut across from margin to margin, to set the oppressed sinner free.

But has it gone to his head? Has he now become a libertine, a profligate? Has he become an anarchist?

Which is lawful on the Sabbath: to do good or to do evil, to save life or to kill? The room is silent. This rabbi has become a new Moses, standing at the brink of a promised land, setting before the people a simple, stark choice.

Life or death.

The rabbi has set before the people a new kind of life, a new kind of humanity. His new name—Son of Man—stands in for the humanity of all women and all men. His life is the life of all humankind. He shows us the life we never thought we could live.

And yet this same life sets him apart from us all. He shows us the life we know we could never live.

This is the paradox of the Son of Man, of his life and his humanity. He at once reflects a humanity more real and more free than we have ever seen and a humanity more different and more radical than we could ever choose.

The Son of Man is choosing life, new life. His reign is the life of humankind, a new life and a new way of being beyond all our hopes and dreams.

Those who stand equally stern before him, those named the Pharisees, leave this place to choose his death.

part three

The Way of Love

So in the midst of all these questions, in the midst of eight years of wandering, I did receive a sign. But it was a sign I never could have expected.

We never can.

This is the story of that sign.

As it happened, the time when I was wrestling most fiercely with my sense of vocation coincided with the time when I began dating the woman I would eventually marry. And as uncertainty so often does, uncertainty began to saturate into every seam of my life.

I use the word *uncertainty* intentionally here, as opposed to a word like, say, *doubt.* At the heart of my wandering was the absence—the negation—of something, rather than its presence. I was looking for what I thought was certainty. What I had was its absence.

Un-certainty.

And so after a long period of dating, after we both knew that this relationship was going to mean something incredibly significant or mean nothing at all, I began to talk to people I trusted about what it means to ask somebody to marry you.

But I framed it in the way we've been taught by endless romantic comedies: *How do I know she is the one?*

Yes, *the one.*

In short, as in all my other wanderings, I was looking for a sign. I framed it in cerebral, intellectual terms: *How do I know?* I was looking for something outside of myself that would make such certainty possible, the certainty of Romeo for Juliet, the certainty of one thing over all others.

No, more than that.

I was looking for something that would make certainty certain. I was looking for the certainty in and around certainty.

I didn't know at the time that such certain certainties are impossible. Finding any certainty in life is hard. Searching for the certainty that is absolute and final and beyond any and all questioning is unbearable.

Yet this was the spinning solipsism in which I found myself. And so, a few days before Christmas Eve, I spent the morning with a close friend. His name is Peter. We spent several hours talking, laughing, going back and forth between jokes and seriousness. I kept wandering around the conversation with questions, questions that I had often asked before, questions that in many ways I refused to have answered. I spent the morning looking for the sign that would make love certain beyond every certainty.

At one point, Peter said to me: *My only advice is to throw your whole self into it.* I remember the words because it seemed to me at the time to be advice that counted for a whole lot more than my present situation. It still seems to me that way.

Throw your whole self into it.

But by the end of the conversation, I could tell that Peter, in his own playfully sarcastic way, was getting, if only a little, exasperated. I kept looking for the sign—*the one*—and I wasn't listening to any answers.

And then he said it. We were walking near our cars in the parking lot, about to go separate ways. He stopped, looked at me deadpan, eye to eye, and said it.

This is what Peter said: *Sometimes the only sign God gives us is the sign we receive at our baptism—and that's the only sign we need. Maybe the only sign you need to know is that you are in the arms of a loving Father.*

He stopped me short with the words. And I can write them down now—verbatim—because I was so speechless that I had to write them down then. I sat alone in my car writing them down on the only scrap of paper I could find.

Here it was. In the midst of all my questions, even the questions that I refused to have answered, in the midst of this wild-goose chase of a million conversations, he stopped me short with the only sign we ever really need. The sign of water overflowing with grace. The sign of a loving-kind embrace.

This was the sign. And it is perhaps the only sign I will ever need. Then. Now. Forevermore.

To stand in the center of this labyrinth, it strikes me now, again, the indelible memory of a sign of water and embrace. Standing in the center, if I turn myself in place and peer into the labyrinth's circuits, I see their everlasting arms surround me. These earthen paths encircling me—brick enmeshed in grass—envelop me in the loving-kind arms of a loving God.

And oh, how bright this path grows from day to day, leaning on the everlasting arms.

When I stand in the center, the arms of this path embrace me. Their love pulls me past certainty into a deeper knowledge, a greater promise. It throws me—my whole self—into its path, whether my questions are answered or not.

And here again is the paradox of the labyrinth, in another form. Before the labyrinth can be a path to walk, it is an open-armed invitation. Its open entrance invites us, calls us, to enter. If the multi-pathed maze is filled with little choices, a series of right choices enmeshed in a tangle of false ones, then the single-pathed labyrinth calls us into a life, a whole life, of trust. This much we already know, the freedom of its trust.

But as much as we might think the unicursal labyrinth is simply blind surrender, no series of choices to be made, it still compels a decision. One momentous decision.

We must decide whether we will enter the labyrinth in the first place.

The labyrinth isn't a path, the journey cannot begin, until the one who would walk it takes the first step. It is a decision not unlike the decision that compelled the speaker in Robert Frost's most famous poem to begin with the famous words: *Two roads diverged in a yellow wood . . .*

One momentous decision.

And it can make all the difference.

In this, the labyrinth can be like life. Life all too often brings us to singular momentous decisions that can make all the difference. Or so it seems.

Thus our uncertainty, our confusion, our fear.

Yet all the labyrinth asks us to do is to trust the invitation. And we can respond to its open arms in one of three ways. We can accept it with our trust. We can decline it with our fear. Or we can simply wander away and around the open invitation, straying here and there, sometimes close, sometimes far away.

For a long time, this was my response. It is a choice that isn't really a choice at all, but rather the postponement of choice. It is like the young lovers on a Saturday afternoon, with a whole night free before them, whose conversation simply bounces back and forth: "I don't know. What do *you* want to do?"

This is what the labyrinth, thus far, has taught me.

For me, so much of the wandering toward and away from a sense of calling was (and maybe still is, if I am honest with myself) rooted in a deep fear of making the wrong choice, a fear of uncertainty, a fear that the certainties I do have aren't worth my trust. What if this isn't what my life is meant to be? What if this isn't what God is calling me to? What will I do then? What do I do now?

How do I know if this is the one?

We can spend so much of our lives in the wilderness of such wandering that all the choices we make aren't really choices at all. They are postponements of choice.

Which means the first step is the hardest step of all. So much so that we may say to enter into the labyrinth is to answer the calling of its path.

The labyrinth calls us, beckons us, invites us into a certain kind of life.

It is, in short, a point of no return.

The paradox of the labyrinth is that even when we make these kinds of momentous decisions, they aren't really decisions at all, or at least they are never as momentous as we often make them out to be. In a sense, the labyrinth offers us a decision that deconstructs our decision making. It defuses our fear of where the decision might leave us. The point of no return is simply the acknowledgment that we can never go back to the past that time, the ever-rolling stream, has already left behind.

In this way, the labyrinth is its own kind of parable. It tells its simple story to cut through our cerebral questions, to break open the mystery at the heart of things. To walk the path of the labyrinth is to walk the way of amazement and wonder, the way of questions that can be answered only with speechless awe. The awe of a crowd before a carpenter prophet. The awe of a leper made clean. Perhaps we may even say that this is the labyrinth's own vocation, to show us again the way beyond simple choices and answers, the holy way of wonder and awe. We take each step to leave behind the past and move into the present moment, its center, into the loving-kind arms that will enfold us there.

Perhaps the most vexing human need is the need for certainty. The need can turn in upon itself, curling in upon itself, until even what we hold to be most certain—the truths we hold self-evident—is not true or certain enough.

The opposite is also true. If my certainties come easily, if they don't challenge me to ask questions of them, if they require nothing of me but my comfortable inertia, then those are exactly the certainties that are most likely to be false.

The way of the labyrinth stretches us to seek something other than certainty. It fills the need for certainty by making us more comfortable with the turns of ambiguity, to, dare I say it, delight in the ambiguity. The labyrinth makes us comfortable with ambiguity by showing us a way through uncertainty and confusion and doubt by a path that we can nonetheless trust. We can delight within the ambiguity because our eyes have been opened to the wonder that we are even given eyes to see, ears to hear, a tongue to ask, a mind to search, a heart to hold.

That is, it shows us the way of love. Love is the one way beyond both certainty and uncertainty. The love whose very being embraces us—our whole self—does not need our certainties. The only sign it needs is the sign of itself, the life it gives to all who are embraced by it. This life overflows us like water, overflowing our whole lives through. This life frees us to love even without certainty. It shows us that the best we are given to do in the face of life's inevitable uncertainties is to love and be loved, to be embraced by the love of everlasting arms.

And it is the only sign we need.

In case you're wondering, a few days later—on Christmas Eve—she answered my question. She said *yes*, without hesitation.

It was a step—one momentous decision—on the way of love.

11

Tree of Life

I WALK THE LABYRINTH IN THE MORNING. The eastern sun has not yet risen above the stonewalled eastern wing of the church building. It juts out to the north from the church sanctuary to make the unshaded right angle of lawn in which the labyrinth sits. It hides the eastern horizon while leaving the west open to full view. This is the particular space of this particular labyrinth.

In the brightening light of a hidden sun, the churchyard is taking on the air of a garden.

For a time in Europe, especially England, from the 1500s to the 1600s, garden labyrinths, made of hedges, were in vogue. They were made as labyrinths of courtly love and affection, for couples to promenade. Fairs and dances would be celebrated around them, a rite of spring.

At the center would stand a maypole, a tree.

It was called the Tree of Life. It stood at the center of the garden. To get to it, one had to walk the labyrinth of love, in love.

This morning I am alone, but I do not walk the way alone. The birds are singing the morning, full throated and alive. But the trees are still a skeletal web against a pale sky, bereft of the flesh of leaves. We remain before the threshold of spring and its rites of love and affection.

I walk the labyrinth in the air of a garden.

I begin to pray the familiar words. They begin in their own address of divine affection.

Our Father, who art in heaven.

The crowds are pressing tighter and tighter against Jesus, almost a mob, almost crushing the air out of his lungs (Mk 3:20-35 NIV). The rumors are rising, uncontrolled and uncontrollable. Propaganda is spreading, with lethal intent. *He is out of his mind. He is possessed.* The name of Beelzebub is voiced, the demon of demons.

Jesus' response to naive misperceptions and sinister half-truths—now and throughout this Gospel—will be mysterious mazes of words. He speaks now in *parables*, puzzling fictions. He speaks in enigmas and paradoxes, proverbs and irony, mind-bending analogies.

He speaks in labyrinths.

He is, if you will, his own kind of Daedalus.

Truly, I tell you. Jesus speaks each syllable slowly. The words refuse to be taken lightly. Depth and gravity are in his voice, from the deepest recesses of his being. Literally, he is speaking *amen* upon his own name, to speak in the power of his own word. His authority comes from the integrated power of his own being—his whole self, his own singular relationship with the One Isaiah called *God of the Amen*—and from no one else.

He is a labyrinth, speaking in labyrinths.

Thus the paradox of him speaking of the *eternal sin* against the Holy Spirit. Generations have wrestled with the mystery of the words. In context, the sin would seem to be to intentionally call good evil and evil good, a slander of the creative order underlying the cosmos. I have heard it said that if one is worried about committing the *eternal sin*, then that is a good indication that one hasn't committed it. But such angst is part of the paradox of following Jesus.

Even still, his piercing deconstruction of those who oppose him is one thing. Piercing his own flesh and blood is quite another. His flesh and blood—his family—stand outside the house. The jammed mass of people will not allow them entrance. And Jesus almost cruelly plays with the tension in this crammed space. Turning to his inner circle, yet speaking loud enough for all to hear, he questions.

Who are my mother and my brothers?

He shows no affection on his face.

The looks he receives back are puzzled. The looks he receives from his family, were he able to see them, are a wounded shock. He had renounced a home for the sake of homelessness. He now renounces a family to become a stranger there.

Here are my mother and my brothers!

He smiles, slyly.

Here too is the paradox of the reign of God. His renunciation becomes the adoption into the family of God of all who do the will of God. Jesus of Nazareth, Son of Man, humanity of humanity, is redrawing the lines of flesh and blood to include the whole genealogy of humankind. He is inviting all humanity into the family of God.

If strength does indeed depend on unity—*a house . . . divided against itself . . . cannot stand*—then this invitation will be the source of the strength of God's reign in the world.

Jesus is making his Father our Father. By his amen, he is inviting all into the loving-kind embrace of the God of the Amen. His reign is extending now to where there is no outsider to his family circle.

Little do his mother and brothers know now how much this painful renunciation will eventually deepen the roots of their own love for this man, deeper than any tie of blood or tribe. Too soon, he will be their brother again, in a way and with a love they could never now know.

I stand in the center of the labyrinth, in the air of the garden.

I stand where the Tree of Life would stand.

I stand in the air of a love I could never now know.

Indeed, only because of the piercing words of the Son of Man can I—at the particular center of this particular labyrinth opening to a westward sky on this particular day—pray in the center of the labyrinth of my soul.

Without it, I would not be able to begin, with divine affection.

Our Father, who art in heaven.

Without it, I would not be able to end.

Amen. Ever and again, to pray *Amen* in his name.

12

Seed

N*IGHT AND DAY*. I walk the labyrinth in the twilight tonight, after dusk, after my son is asleep. Except the sky is pocked by clouds; there is no starlight by which to see. But the twilight glows the luminous sky just enough, and the city gives off just enough streetlight, that I can make out inky lines in gray grass.

I narrow my eye, fixed to the gray ground as I walk. The darkness forces me to concentrate on the maze's path in a way the day does not.

The kingdom of God is as if . . .

The parables have given the story a newfound regular rhythm (Mk 4:26-34). A regular beat. And there is a marvelous simplicity to these little stories. In them we discern the obvious. "But of course the seed grows of itself," we hear ourselves say. Almost as if we knew it all along.

But if the kingdom is as obvious as a seed in springtime, what is so new about it?

Even though the revelation of it feels ancient, primordial, there is nothing we could have known about it except by the voice of the Son of Man. The kingdom he comes to bring by the very words of his mouth grows new and fresh on its own. At the heart of it is mystery. It cannot be cultivated nor manufactured.

At the heart of all knowledge is mystery. The mystery of a seed in springtime.

It cannot be forced or coerced or sought after. It simply *happens.* Wherever it happens, it happens by the spark of its own self-generating power.

As apparent as it seems, it is far from obvious.

Night and day . . . the earth produces of itself.

This earth too is sprouting of itself new life in spring. I cannot see it, but it is happening: *first the stalk, then the head, then the full grain in the head.* The cycle of the earth's life is coming back around to its youthfulness. I cannot describe it, but I can feel it in the air. Birth and rebirth. Night and day, the seed grows, new blades green. Night and day, the labyrinth of a seed sits in a spiral of earth. Whether I sleep or I rise, it is here.

As I walk my way out of the labyrinth, I am startled by a rabbit sprinting across my way. There are lives who walk this path in the night and in the day—unknown to me—part of the sacred mystery of a seed.

As I leave in the late darkness, light illuminates an upper room in the church. For what I do not know. A council meeting? A Bible study? An AA group? The pastor working?

The kingdom of God produces of itself.

The center of the labyrinth is its seed. From its husk—its smallest circle—the circuits sprout and expand into large branches, circuits of time and space. For those who make nests in its path, the time and space are made sacred. It expands the sacred gift of time and space, bending into every moment and place.

The seed is its own labyrinth. Curled within its microscopic husk is all the life it will need to become the flower, the shrub, the tree. It is the earth's dynamo of life growing unto life. And it will generate the fruit of life full grown to become the seed again, from sowing to sprouting to harvest to sowing once more.

Night and day. Birth and rebirth.

As I walk home, I remember being the child who plants the seed of a flower in a cup and places it on the sill. I remember being the child who watches over it, night and day. I remember it growing. And I remember the mystery of the growing, from stalk to head to flower. But I never saw it growing, never caught it in the movement of the act.

It simply happened, I knew not how.

I am still that child. I know not how.

Along the way, I am met by the sylvan scent of incense heavy in the air, coming from I know not where. It imparts mystery to the evening. Lights from within homes glow the neighborhood. Life is hidden in these husks of brick and wood, to sprout again when day returns. I come to my home, lit from within. I stand before the door. There is life hidden there—the love of my life, the life of my love—moving within it as within a seed.

My love stirs through the house. My child slumbers.

It happens, I know not how.

With what can we compare the kingdom of God? It is like a child who sleeps and wakes, eats and plays. Parents protect him in their waking hours. But he sprouts and grows, we know not how, chattering his life in new revelations of life. "But of course the child grows." That much is obvious. But we know not how, except by the voice of the One who creates the child's life, the source of his childlike wonder. The child grows from the smallest of life into a life all his own.

There will be no other life like this child's life. The surprise of laughter is in his lungs and the tenderness of love is in his hands.

I stand at the door, in darkness, and all this happens. The seed is planted in the earth of my heart. It grows. It produces of itself. I know not how.

13

Children

EVENING HAS COME TO ANOTHER LONG DAY (Mk 4:35-41). The sky is pocked with clouds. There is no starlight to see by. Jesus' face is ragged and worn, like fraying linen. His voice is low and hoarse, like dry wind scraping gravel. *Let us go across to the other side.*

I walk the labyrinth again, the morning after last night, only to discover that there are schedules this churchyard keeps outside of my own. Parents are bringing children to the church as I arrive. They are bringing them to the church's preschool. Nevertheless, I walk the labyrinth amid this procession of parents and children, trying to remain as discreet as possible. When my path bends close to theirs, I greet the parents I see with a smile. But for the most part I keep my head down, scanning the ground before my feet.

The morning air is warm. It will be warm for a few more hours before a cold front comes through, one more echo of winter.

It strikes me that were I able to look down from the sky on the ground before my feet, the lines of the labyrinth would look something like the hurricane on a weather map, spirals circling in and out of the eye of the storm. As I reach the center, I notice that the ground at the heart of the center of the labyrinth is growing worn and bare. It is the pupil of the eye of the storm, the only place in the stormy maze where one stands still.

I stand in the center, self-conscious before the procession. I keep my eyes on the bare spot of ground where I stand. My lips are closed.

I pray, silently, my lips closed.

卐

Let us go across to the other side. The disciples stare into darkness down to the ground before their feet. They keep their heads down because they know *the other side* leads to a frontier heretofore unexplored.

The Gentiles.

Jesus' face is ragged and worn. He is dead tired. He leans on the companions at his side, his arms reaching around their shoulders. They buckle themselves to anticipate the burden of his load. But he feels weightless, almost as if he were lifting them. They bring him to rest in the boat—*just as he was*—and he falls deeply asleep, immediately. *Just as he was*—they behold this man, exhausted yet lithe. His head nods to the side, knocking the center plank of the boat.

For this one night at least there will be rest upon the water.

One of them retrieves a cushion and, cupping Jesus' heavy head in his hands, lays the pillow under it. As Jesus sleeps, he dreams visions unknown, a frontier unexplored.

The rest on the water is short-lived. Heavy drops of water begin to splatter the floorboards. The still surface of water is broken. The sea is troubled by rain. The air is troubled by thunder.

Not that there is anything evil in the thunderheads now raining wind and wave upon the lake. There is nothing in the Gospel of Mark to indicate that there is some kind of sinister violence in the weather. Nevertheless, the fear is palpable, knotting the disciples' throats. Deep fear gasps the air from their lungs. *Teacher, do you not care that we are perishing?*

Jesus' unknown dream is broken by screaming. It comes from every direction of the sea.

He rises quickly and leaps to the stern of the boat. He stands there tall and rigid, arms outstretched in a benevolent rage, and he talks to the wind. He *rebuked* the wind. The heavens warp and bend to a circle around the Son of Man, pleading in a whirling whine. The Son of Man speaks in reply.

They speak to each other in primeval syllables, a language the disciples cannot discern through the roar.

Until the final word.

Peace!

The word is spoken to the storm, but it is a word for them all, every life within earshot.

Peace! Be still!

Only now do we see that the authority of this man is a cosmic power. It is the power of the sublime, beyond the artistry of words. It elicits a speechless mixture of wonder, then awe, then dread terror. As much as his companions cowered before the waves, they now cower before the sopped man who slumps back into the hull before them. Water drips in rivulets from his bowed head.

Why are you afraid? His voice is hoarse again. But the second rebuke is more severe than the first.

The sea is smooth as glass. The air is still. The land on the other side is in view. Dawn is rising with warm morning air.

Daedalus's design was true. The path of the labyrinth is the passage to and from trouble and pain, wind and wave, the passage we pray our children to be spared. It is the tortuous path to protect us from evil. Yet it is the inevitable path of a world broken and suffering. The only way to arrive at the still eye of the storm is to pass through the storm. This much is true.

There is a seventeenth-century book from Nuremberg, Germany, that carries an engraving of Daedalus's Cretan labyrinth. The book is a catechism, a religious guide for children, a guide to learn safe passage in a torturous world. At the center of the labyrinth engraving is the monster Minotaur, half man, half beast. The monster remains trapped within the maze of walls. Beyond the labyrinth, in the distance, is a sailboat sailing away, sailing freely on open water.

In the Nuremberg catechism, the engraving of the labyrinth of Daedalus is used to illuminate the seventh petition of the Lord's Prayer.

Deliver us from evil.

So here, standing silently still, standing on bare ground in the eye of the storm, I pray.

Deliver us from evil.

Deliver us all—all children, all of us children—deliver us from evil.

14

In Peace

SO SOON, BITTERNESS BITES THE COLD air again. Midnight was warmer than this noontime.

Nevertheless I walk my daily walk.

I can't help but feel that we will never leave behind the cold, this reverberating chill. The emerging flowers and shrubs—not yet in bloom—shiver under a steely gray sky.

卐

So soon, the circle surrounding Jesus is sailing back again, away from the other side (Mk 5:21-43 NIV). In the boat, Jesus has turned his face back toward Galilee.

But his disciples still face back to the other shore, silent and wondering. The desperate, frantic pleading of the young man they left behind still echoes in their ears. Now they are in deep water, but the bloated carcasses of swine lapping against the hull along the shore haunt their memory.

So soon, they will reach the shore of Galilee, familiar ground. But it will be many nights before images of the Gerasenes will leave their troubled sleep.

卐

I walk briskly and feel my body—shoulders, neck, arms, hands—shrugging in upon itself to stay warm. How much colder the cold always feels after warmth has come and left. At the center, I pray quickly the prayer that answers the plea: *O Lord, remember us in your kingdom and teach us to pray.* By the end of my circuit back out of the labyrinth, I can think of nothing else than of how cold I have become. My bare face feels like ice.

My little daughter is dying. A man named Jairus is pleading with Jesus within the crowd along the road in Galilee.

It is striking that only now, along this road in Galilee, does a woman take center stage in Mark's drama. She enters as an interruption. A woman touches the man's cloak with her hidden silence because she cannot openly approach him. *She had suffered a great deal under the care of many doctors and had spent all she had.* Our world may have changed from hers, but the predicament is strikingly real, strikingly present. She might as well be wearing jeans and a sweater, her past-due medical bill in hand.

But her faith is as uncommon in our day as in hers.

If I just touch his clothes, I will be healed.

She cowers at the sound of his voice. Trembling, she makes herself known, a woman before a man in a man's world. The push of the crowd pushes them close together, face to face, eye to eye. She tells him the whole truth and truth alone.

Daughter, he whispers.

She can smell what's left of figs on his sweet breath. *Your faith has healed you. Go in peace and be freed from your suffering.* She who was brought low is now raised up—face to face, eye to eye—standing with the Son of Man, the human within humanity.

He is still speaking as another voice breaks through the crowd.

Your daughter is dead.

Standing beside Jesus, Jairus slumps. His head drops below his shoulders.

Jesus is undaunted by the news. His speaking does not halt. Peace continues to roll in whispers off his tongue. *Don't be afraid; just believe.* His words are for the woman as much as the man, just as they were for the man as much as the woman. They all stand close and eye to eye.

Your faith has healed you. Go in peace and be freed. Don't be afraid. Just believe.

Jairus believes, but in what he does not know. His belief, like the woman's, consists in only one thing. He trusts the Son of Man. He follows after him. Their belief is the sheer act of sole trust, thrown in with their whole self. Their eyes are fixed on him whose words are comfort, whose touch is power. All else slides away.

Later, after the little girl's mother has given her *something to eat,* she will run out the door of the house to play before dark. And as the disciples sit around an empty table, staring at the Son of Man, there will be only one response. Speechless awe. The syllables of the question asked time and again—*who is this?*—will echo in their minds. They will echo in the air mixed within the siren of crickets, the whir of a locust.

After leaving the labyrinth, I walk down the hill, across the street. I enter Winslow's Home. Inside, it is warm. My muscles unravel again in the warmth. I sit at an empty table, with an empty mind, waiting for something to eat. I sit at the empty table in my own kind of speechless awe.

The food fortifies me whole. I will walk out this door astonished by the warm pulse of new life. Jesus' words are for me as much as they were for the two who stood so close to him as to smell his breath.

I go in peace.

I am free.

I am not afraid.

I believe.

15

Passage

IT SNOWED THIS MORNING.

In the sky, the clouds plaster a ceiling in the sky, solid and unyielding. On land, the thin sheet of snow illuminates the emerald green of the grass, articulate strokes of pigment against white paper. I had not noticed how green the grass had become in this slow time, except now by snow. Likewise, the snow is more accustomed to covering a dormant earth, stripped and drab.

This ground is awakened and alive, breaking through the sparkling frost.

This is the beautiful paradox of snow in spring. This is the paradox of hope.

The light snow has brought out the beautiful, stark symmetry of the labyrinth's design, its art: russet red lines encircling white-speckled green.

My breath fogs before my eyes, then dissipates. The wind has died. So the air is pleasantly cold. My steps are cautious and halting in the slant of the yard. I fear slipping. My shoes leave slush prints behind me in the wafer sheet of snow.

Jesus left that place and came to his hometown. I remember how lonely I felt the first time I returned home from college fifteen years ago, how small the house I grew up in seemed when I returned. I remember how lost I felt three years ago when we crossed half the country to move here from the place that had become our home, even though this place is the place I was born.

What do we do when a hometown no longer feels like home?

What to do when a familiar place is rendered strange?

This is how time meddles with place. The people who stay in one place are changed one way by time. Those who move to another are changed another way. When those who leave return, all are changed, but by divergent paths. And no one can say exactly what changed. Even when we all know it has. All is different; only the space remains.

And yet the space changes too.

Nothing can be the same.

The circle of companions arrives home as strangers (Mk 6:1-13). Neighbors look at them without a hint of recognition. Childhood friends step back to look them up and down before their old memories return. They are not the same as when they left. Nobody is the same. Everything has diverged along paths, a maze expanding outward but with boomerang force.

The companions do not admit it to each other, but often when they see their own reflection, they themselves no longer recognize the weather-beaten face they see there.

Jesus and his circle have returned to a familiar place rendered strange. The events encircling the sea—tempest, torment, miracle, resurrection—have made all things strange. People here seem to remember them only in former terms: fishermen, cousins, hagglers.

And a carpenter turned would-be prophet.

The people would rather have the domesticity of a carpenter than the wild ferocity of a prophet. *Prophets are not without honor, except in their hometown.* The disciples can hear the shutting of doors as they walk the streets, shutting them out, unwelcomed. Amazement turns to indignation.

In their own hometown, they have become homeless.

So the carpenter turned prophet leaves.

He leaves the same way he came, a second line of footprints in the thin sheet of dust. He leaves for the surrounding villages, to be received again for who he now is. And he sends out his Twelve, to become what they soon shall be. He sends them with the Spirit with which he is sent. He sends them with power, and power alone. *No bread. No bag. No money in their belts.* And, to those who would receive them as someone they are not, an instruction.

Shake off the dust that is on your feet. You are not at home here.

The reign of God is a maze expanding outward with boomerang force. Those on diverging paths will circle back to the One who stands at the center. They will proclaim repentance. They will cast out demons. They will anoint with oil. From their hands, the Spirit will release and heal.

Homeless, they will find a place in this ever-moving center, this inbreaking of God.

In time long gone, the labyrinth was an embodiment of initiation rites, the passage of life in time, of growth, of the movement from one stage to another. It is the passage from the end of what has passed to the beginning of what is new.

The commencement at the end of the journey.

The labyrinth embodies, literally, the rite of passage. It passes us from one age to the next, the turns of time stepped into in the space of a path. And then out again.

The circle of the labyrinth is the image simultaneously of both the clock and the compass, the instrument that measures time and and the one that measures space.

At the center—where time and space stop—is the death of former things and the rebirth of what is new. The one who exits the labyrinth, even though her steps tread the same path, is different from the one who entered it. The path is the same but the steps are reversed. Thus, the vantage points are completely changed. The lines of sight are utterly new. This then is how the heart changes, the path of *metanoia*: to see the same space with new eyes, to walk the same places with new steps.

Perhaps this is why the earliest labyrinths, dating from the Bronze Age (ca. 2000 B.C.E.), are figures connected to graves or mines. They were emblems for those places where people—dead or alive—return to the earth. They are narrow paths fraught with danger, passages into the unknown, into risk, into the threat that one may not return to the surface. Thus, to return along these same passages is to be reborn, to be made alive again into someone new.

It is the strange passage into the homelessness of a new beginning.

Lost in thought, I reach the center in timeless intimation, amid questions. Is this my home? Where is home?

And the one question that hasn't changed: What do I seek?

This center space, where I stand in place, this is—for one moment—my home. For the time being. For this time in space, space in time. Home is where this heart is, reborn. Winding around the vortex of me, I can trace my walk in wet footsteps—gray prints in the white-speckled green—a singular path weaving in circles until it reaches where I now stand.

On my way back around, I leave a second set of footsteps. At the entrance which is the exit, I survey the whole. Two divergent roads treading the same ground.

And again, the familiar place is rendered strange.

Time meddles with place once again. It makes all the difference.

I cannot say what changed, but nothing remains the same.

16

As Yet Untrodden

IT IS SNOWING AGAIN. But this time not a dusting. It is coming down in fat, wet white clumps. The outline of the world is traced in white slush. The snow sharpens every wrinkle of tree, every slant of architecture, every crevice of surface, into high relief. Despite its unwelcome arrival, it will make for a beautiful cityscape.

I have to lower my face to look at my feet to be able to see through the white downpour. There are two inches on the ground as I approach the labyrinth. But there are faint lines in the snow. I take my walk as a test. And I seem to know the way. Somewhere in the recesses of memory, I know how to walk the mazy path, even without clear sight.

Only when I reach the center do my footprints tell me that I have not walked the whole path. There is a circuit I missed by missing a turn. Its path is blank snow, a path as yet untrodden. Yet somehow I still reached the center. The labyrinth forgave my transgression. My sight, my memory—in the labyrinth, in life—is yet imprecise.

King Herod. As Mark tells the story we wouldn't yet know it, but he is a paranoid despot (Mk 6:14-29). An impetuous madcap. A terrorizing chieftain. He is driven by the passions of the moment, whether the wonder of prophets, the desires of a dance, the foreboding of oaths, the grief of death.

King Herod heard of it, for Jesus' name had become known. Jesus has walked along the borderlands and margins, but the word of him now reaches palace and tower, a center of power. And only now does Mark's story let us in on what has been an open secret.

The incarceration of John the Baptizer. His crime: to speak truth to power.

His sentence becomes death despite the king's fascination. The head on the plate pales to blue, its open mouth finally silent, thick tongue plopped on mirrored silver. An unrecognizable reflection. The garnishes surrounding John's head—grapes, olives, and fig leaves—are the stewards' vicious stab at parody. The courtiers snicker. Herod is silent.

The fact that the Gospel has delayed this account until now—in this, Mark's most famous intercalation—heightens our terror. We receive it as a flashback. We had forgotten of the forerunner John, forgotten in our amazement of the One he baptized into a new journey for us all. John had receded into a distant memory.

Little did we know until now.

And to hear it now is to hear it as a threat against the One John foreran. To know now that news of his acts has reached the throne of an obsessed executioner gives us more than pause. This despot will not cede power to the powerless, nor to those who threaten his power. His power rests on others' powerlessness. And it rests on what he does to those who threaten his power.

This is the logic of tyranny. Already one prophet's lifeless head, its speechless mouth agape, sits on a platter. What will Herod do with the other?

I walk the labyrinth after attending a memorial service. I am still in my charcoal suit, my overcoat, my black dress shoes. The shoes and my pant legs are soaked through with melted snow. The snow has penetrated my soles. My feet are wet and growing cold.

I am thinking about death. Cruel cold death, claiming the head of the Baptist. Cruel cold death, claiming the life of one too early. But the echoing psalm of the congregation still sings in my path.

The King of love my shepherd is,
Whose goodness faileth never;
I nothing lack if I am his
And he is mine forever.

I am thinking about death. And about resurrection. *John, whom I beheaded, has been raised.* In actuality, Herod's conviction is a mystical delusion. But in another sense, Herod speaks truth. Despite every tyranny, prophets will still rise. Their truth will still speak. Their power will still free the powerless.

The darkness cannot hide the light.

When his disciples heard about it, they came and took his body, and laid it in a tomb. There is a quiet solemnity to the act. John's disciples do not speak as they lift the body from the butcher's table. They unhook the shackles on his feet and hands, cleanse the wounds where sharp iron met skin. They do not speak as they anoint the corpse. With what little they have left, they bargain for a whole linen cloth. Tenderly, they wrap the body in it. They lay it in the tomb, the husk of a seed in hope to rise again. It is quiet, ominous, as they stand around the tomb, still sweating, still exhausted by the work of grief.

One of them sings softly the psalm.

And so through all the length of days
Thy goodness faileth never;
Good Shepherd, may I sing thy praise
Within thy house forever.

It is quiet, ominous, as one story, one life, ends in the middle of another. Ironically, the Gospel According to Mark will never name the name of Herod Antipas again. But his shadow now looms over all.

As I leave the churchyard, the untrodden circuit of snow signals a more precise memory. It is the memory of a prayer, a prayer spoken in evening prayer, a prayer spoken at the edge of darkness. *O God, you have called your servants to ventures of which we cannot see the ending, by paths as yet untrodden, through perils unknown. Give us faith to go out with good courage, not knowing where we go, but only that your hand is leading us and your love supporting us; though Jesus Christ our Lord. Amen.*

I pray the prayer by memory after I pray the Lord's Prayer. I pray it as I walk my way away from the center, walking the circuits to the exit. It is the memory of a prayer for the labyrinth of life, a prayer for those who still see dimly, imprecisely, a prayer for those who seek what they do not know to find.

I turn back. The one circuit, unstepped before, now bears my prints in the snow. I have trod an untrodden path.

This day, this is all I know for certain on earth, and all I need to know.

part four

Calling, by Name

I said before that there is a way that the labyrinth brings us out of the past and into the present moment. That much is true. But there is also a way in which the labyrinth brings the past into the present moment. The past is always present, in our memories, in our influences, in the way our present thoughts and actions bear forth the past, for better and for worse.

There is this timelessness in time, that in the ever-passing present moment the past we know mixes with the future that is yet coming to be. This is part of the difference in treading the untrodden path, the way the past is thrown forward, the way the future circles back, the way of the present suspended in the restlessness of time. This is the spiral of time.

I mention it because even after I received the sign of a precious word from a good friend, a word that I will never forget, it would still be almost four years before this particular tension would be resolved in the calling of my life.

Perhaps you could say that such incessant wrestling only reflects the discontented restlessness of youth. And perhaps you'd be right. But it could also reflect the spirit of the times in which we live, the end of an old century, the beginning of the new. Perhaps it reflects the restless spirit of time itself, past within present within future.

It is in that spirit that I ask this question, a simple question about the story of time.

Where were you on September 11?

I am quite certain this will be my American generation's great question of time, much like Pearl Harbor was for the Greatest Generation, or the assassination of John F. Kennedy for baby boomers. This will be the question by which we tell the story of our time.

So this is where I was on September 11, 2001, or at least as I remember it now, the past bleeding into the fabric of this present moment. As I remember it, the morning in St. Louis was not unlike the morning as it was in New York City. Clear, sunny, crisp but warm. A sky so blue. The kind of day when the furnace heat of summer breaks into the cooler temperance that tells me autumn is coming.

But it wasn't yet cool enough that I needed a jacket. I remember that.

And it was three months, plus a couple of weeks, from my wedding day.

I was just pulling into the parking lot of the suburban office building where I worked when the morning radio host reported that a plane had struck the World Trade Center. That was the only detail she had. I walked through the door, up the stairs and into my cubicle knowing—as we all did—that there had to be more to the story.

I remember that it was impossible to do much work that day. Not here. Not anywhere. Except at Ground Zero, where we saw people working harder than anyone had ever worked before.

I remember walking around the office, asking for news and answering when I was asked. For most of us, it was too unbearable to sit still. In retrospect, it is hard to remember that this was before social media. There was no Twitter feed. I can remember keeping a window open on my computer to the *New York Times* website, compulsively refreshing it every minute or two. Even then, the news felt so slow.

It didn't take long before there were televisions in several different conference rooms. People were beginning to congregate, to watch a tragedy played out in real time. Minutes turned to hours.

It didn't take long before the executive director called me into his office with a simple request. Plan and lead a prayer service for our staff. We will meet in the chapel at noon.

Funny how it happened. We had about a half-dozen ordained pastors on staff, including my boss, who was also the staff chaplain. All of them were out of the officc that day. So it was left to me to plan a prayer service in the midst of a tragedy that was happening a thousand miles away and yet was devastating us all.

Funny how quickly we may have forgotten how empty everything felt that day, how empty we felt. I remembered that day remembering the fragment of a line by T. S. Eliot that haunted me for months afterward: *A heap of broken images.* When the first tower fell, my mind was a heap of broken images, wondering how to lead us into prayer together when everything felt so empty.

And then the moment struck like an epiphany.

It came with the humble realization that my job was not to pray on behalf of these people, my coworkers, my friends. My job was to provide the time and the space—the open welcome—so that we might speak our prayers together to God. Everything came into its place from there. At noon, we sang hymns and sacred songs, we spoke a litany, we read psalms. And we prayed. Oh, how we prayed together. We groaned to God our words of sadness, and those prayers were returned to us as comfort we could share, a gift of daily bread.

And I remember this. I remember it in the vivid colors of light refracted through the chapel's stained glass. I remember standing before these people—my coworkers, my friends—with my arms outstretched as we held hands together to pray the prayer taught to us to pray—the Lord's Prayer—and I remember the thought entering my mind as a gift, the pure and simple grace of a gift: *to this, and for this moment, I have been called.*

As I remember it now, this became my first step into the labyrinth. In the midst of all the wrestling and questions, all the wandering away and around its open invitation, all the uncertainty, the confusion, the fear of a tragic day that could never have felt more uncertain, confusing or fearful, this was my first sure step into the labyrinth of my calling.

Sometimes the sense of calling we feel is rooted deep enough to last a lifetime. Sometimes it lasts for only a moment, a wisp in the wind. Sometimes it is both at the same time. But once we take that first step, however that first step takes shape, the path of the labyrinth turns from invitation to vocation, to the life to which we are called.

Our sense of a life's purpose, of what we call our *calling*, has its roots in the Latin verb *vocare* and the noun *vocatio*, from which we get the English word *vocation*. In the Latin, *vocare* simply means "to call," but it carries the further connotations of "to name," "to invoke." Thus, *vocare* is not only the specific callings upon our lives but also the way our lives are given a name, and the invocation upon which it both receives blessing and imparts blessing to others.

So many of the callings, the vocations, of my life are given to me before I could even know it, and how they are given to me is beyond my control. I am born as a child to parents, and maybe a sibling to siblings. I become a student to teachers.

And yet other callings imply a choice. I study and prepare for a job, a profession, a career. I commit myself to a partner, and she commits herself to me. We deliberate and plan for if, how and when to become parents to children.

And this, I think, is where we can get caught in the middle, in between the callings we feel we have chosen and the callings that are beyond our control. And in the tensions of all these things, we look for some semblance of certainty.

We still look for signs.

We can spend so much of our lives looking for signs, signs to tell us which way to go, clear signs from God for what to do with our lives. And yet all our sign-seeking is just a more complicated form of bargaining in the face of our fear. We want to know every single turn in the path before we take the first step.

Thus we turn the sign-seeking into platitudes, into clichés. And our lives can become simply a procession from one pious cliché to another, seeking order to spite the disorder. When I was a child and I happened to be sick on a Sunday, my parents would have me watch *The Hour of*

Power from Robert Schuller's famous Crystal Cathedral. In hindsight, I think they did it so I would know I couldn't fake my way out of church. And at the time, the Crystal Cathedral was the only church on TV, the only church that could turn our living-room sofa into a pew, whether I was really sick or just faking it.

At the time, it wasn't hard to be inspired by the spirituality Schuller so eloquently evoked, the way he made things seem so clear and plain. But inevitably, their meaning for me would fade. We can chart the history of our lives by the spiritual clichés with which we live them. Whether it is Schuller's "power of positive thinking," or "the purpose-driven life," or "your best life now," ad infinitum, we can chart our spiritual lives with the clichés by which we live them.

The problem is those clichés so quickly wear out, *a heap of broken images*. And so we need to find a new platitude, over and over again, feigning a feeble order in the latest cliché of our lives.

The way, the *vocare*, of the labyrinth turns such piety on its head. The labyrinth orders disorder not by the straight line of the cliché but by the unending circle of a paradox. It makes its way not by stringing tight the shortest distance from one point to another, but by finding the longest way possible to get from the entrance to the end. It orders disorder by imitating disorder, by finding a holy artistry in life's accidents, by designing chaos.

Which is why the center of the labyrinth is empty, a void. It is empty not so that we can fill it with whatever pious platitudes are trending this moment, but so that it can mirror the emptiness of all our pieties, the disorder inherent in the order we try to make of it, the chaos in our feeble plans.

And then it asks us—simply—to open our eyes. To walk into the *vocare* of the labyrinth is to open our eyes to the wondrous gift of this path of a day, of the way one fleeting moment can break into timeless epiphany. *To this, and for this moment, I have been called.* The *vocare* of the labyrinth is to follow, with all our broken images, the calling of this mysterious carpenter-prophet from Galilee, whose every word and every deed is the opening up to something new.

I once heard someone say—I can't remember who—that most of us, even most religious people, live by a "practical atheism." We believe in God. But we live as if God doesn't exist. The belief has no bearing on our everyday existence. And our view of who God is—immovable mover, bad cop, distant father—makes no practical difference to how we spend our days, because the god we have in view is merely an extension of what we either want or fear God to be. We look for that extraordinary moment when God seems to intervene in human affairs, in exactly the way we expect God will, and we call it a miracle. But we blithely overlook the ways the divine is saturated within the minutest details of our routines, the minutiae, bleeding into the fabric of the present moment. We fail to see the sheer miracle of the way the move of the sun slants light to reveal something changed, the way a blade of grass is reborn green in spring, the way our daily experiences are ripening into a wisdom we didn't know we had.

We fail to see these things because of the way such seeing might change the whole way we live, because, I think, we're scared that it may call us to risk everything we thought we wanted for something completely unknown.

In short, it calls us to see and hear and taste a God beyond cliché, the God of labyrinths, the God who makes art within accidents, the God hidden in *a heap of broken images.* This is the same God of whom Luther wrote: "Nothing is so small but God is still smaller, nothing is so large but God is still larger, nothing is so short but God is still shorter, nothing is so long but God is still longer, nothing is so broad but God is still broader, nothing is so narrow but God is still narrower, and so on. He is an inexpressible being, above and beyond all that can be described or imagined."

This is the God concealed and revealed in paradox. When we behold this God, we see from the eyes of the cosmos that all this time we measure is, as a wise preacher once wrote, really one day, and it is only this world—sunrise to sunset—that is turning within it. When we behold this God, our arms outstretched, we are given the gift of this grace. It calls us by name. It invokes blessing upon our lives, received and given away. The gift hides in our heaping brokenness, bleeds into its fabric and fills our emptiness with newfound wholeness. It fills us to a fullness flowing over.

To this, and for this moment, I have been called.

And twelve baskets will not be enough to gather up what is left over from one day, one moment, of this grace.

17

Petals

THE SNOW IS GONE, except for a few patches sitting under shadow. It fast-melted yesterday, falling from trees in heavy clumps. A second snowfall from earth to earth.

Overnight fell below freezing for the second night in a row, risking the death of plants that sprang too early. I am no gardener, but I am anxious about the peonies on the side of our house. Yesterday, I pushed new tomato cages—a labyrinth of wire, concentric circles spiraling upward—into the earth around them so that they might grow tall, weaving the maze. The peonies had broken the hard ground, thick purple stalks. They have risked death by their revelation, by breaking open what was formerly hidden under earth. But they risk death because they have been betrayed by the season, by what should be the sure clockwork of a nature much larger than themselves.

This morning, I arrive at the moment when the long shadow of a church gable stabs through the heart of the labyrinth. It is cold but the air is bright with sunlight. I know I should see my breath, but it fleets away with the sideways wind. It is cold, but the cold is thin. No longer the deep freeze of midwinter, but the thin frost of a spring slumbering late to its equinox.

A handful of forsaken petals strew the labyrinth, pale white and magenta, the colors of bread and wine. Tulip petals perhaps. Or perhaps from the blooming tree next to the street. Or perhaps remnants from a weekend wedding. Now they lie wet and limp, glued to brick, matted flat against matted grass.

The cold may be thin, but it penetrates my clothes. I walk briskly and do not stay long. I long for the leisure of spring, the warmth that allows for lingering, the length of day.

The disciples return from their tours with success (Mk 6:30-44). Thus the Gospel According to Mark now calls them, for the first time, *apostles*, witnesses to the reign of God breaking forth in the world. Only now, after long days of work—with *no leisure even to eat*—there is *rest*. They board the boat again with time to themselves.

Except that this rest too will be cut short by coming and going, by hurried feet, by *sheep without a shepherd*. The rest is, as it always seems, cut short.

This is a deserted place, and the hour is now very late. The prophet scans the peopled shore and beckons his circle back to work. He extends the invitation. *You give them something to eat.* This is the work of apostles in the reign of God.

Their faces display their stunned skepticism. What they have will scarcely feed themselves, let alone a hungry mob of five thousand hungry men. With women. And children.

Despite the skepticism, despite even themselves, they gather together what daily bread is there.

Five, and two fish.

The loaves and the fish sit in the basket like a handful of forsaken petals.

In the golden glow of dusk, Jesus takes up a loaf of bread. Its grains glimmer in golden light. He looks up into the deep sky and lifts the loaf in two hands, suspended between earth and heaven. He blesses the bread with a word. In his hands, the bread descends back down to the height of his heart. He breaks the loaf. He hands the pieces to his stewards to break again for the people.

And again. And again. And again.

The breaking of bread is unending, thousand upon thousand times over.

The apostles distribute the food to the masses, stewards of a banquet set upon green grass in an otherwise barren wilderness.

The people eat to their fill, with food left over.

How striking is this banquet in contrast to the lavish carousing of Herod. Pleasant sounds arise from this throng, the gentle sounds of table conversation. Pleasantries turn into genuine encounter, a melody of small talk, storytelling, jokes, hearty laughter.

Strangers are becoming friends.

Sitting at the top of a knoll, eating to his own fill, the host of the meal smiles in benediction. These thousands have accepted the invitation.

For all who gather here, the memory of this meal—its emergent miracle—will bless all the meals yet to come. It will be the grace at their table.

And the second miracle is as powerful as the first.

This is the second miracle: amid such a crowd, there is no hoarding at the table. No one fills their satchel with leftover bread. No one hides fish away in their clothes. The food is shared to all. The food is shared by all.

This food is shared to the poor, by the poor, for the poor, all to share.

Thus we are the ones left to ask. What happened to the *twelve baskets* left over?

The Gospel doesn't say. But it foreshadows what will become a tradition among the earliest followers of Jesus. Wherever they gathered to remember the meal, they gathered for Eucharist. And after the sharing of Eucharist—bread broken again and again and again—the leftover food was gathered and distributed to those who could not come to the table.

The Gospel doesn't say. But such hospitalities had to begin somewhere. They had to begin in the memory of a meal—its emergent miracle—the grace at their table.

The memory begins here, with twelve baskets carried and shared from a table of green grass, a harvest in the wilderness.

Twelve baskets shared with those who could not join at the table.

Twelve baskets carried, without price, into towns or along the road.

Twelve baskets shared at family tables and parish halls.

Twelve baskets carried to food pantries and soup kitchens.

Twelve baskets without price, to all with need.

The Gospel doesn't say. But this is the second miracle: the loaves and the fish are multiplying still, even in a cold springtime that risks death, here, now, the gift of daily bread.

18

The Sea

I HAVE BEEN OVER THIS GROUND BEFORE.

This far into my journey, the churchyard feels familiar, commonplace. Likewise, the day is nondescript and overcast. Gray light with no shadow.

It is a Tuesday, like any other Tuesday.

But here is the difference: all along this journey, I have been seeking something, not knowing what. Now, there grows a new awareness.

I seek, but I seek what I know I do not know. A subtle difference, nearly indiscernible: from not knowing to knowing that you do not know. For Socrates, this is the beginning of wisdom, the end of curiosity, the key to discovery.

I seek what I know I do not know.

This far into the journey, this is all I need to know.

I have been over this ground before.

And so I walk the labyrinth as if it were a map, familiar territory, commonplace. It is a map, guiding a journey to its destination. I walk it as if it were a map of Mark's Gospel. All the places along the map's way—this Galilee—come to my mind. Here is Nazareth. Then comes Capernaum. I turn out again into the Judean countryside, unnamed villages and towns. Back again through Capernaum. I skirt along the edge of the sea. Then cross to the country of the Gerasenes. Then turn to come back again, back to Capernaum, then forward farther into Galilee. I am walking the geography of the labyrinth with a clue of thread from the Gospel of Mark.

The labyrinth is my map.

At the center is the sea and its pull, magnetic. Always drawn to the sea. I am standing on the surface of the sea as if on solid ground, as on the peak of a hill. Everything I see looks familiar, even if what is known is unknown, unknowable.

I pray. Known words spoken within the unknown.

We have been over this ground before (Mk 6:45-56). We are back to the sea. But before Jesus climbs into the boat, he will ascend to the peak of the hill—a labyrinth walk all its own—to pray. Alone. No one knows of this communion with his Father. Only he, alone, standing in the center of the hill. He sends his companions ahead of him into their future. From here he can see them—tiny ants—along the shoreline, heaving the boat into the circle of sea.

We have been over this ground before.

What is it about the sea that draws us in?

I remember living a few miles from Long Island Sound. I remember feeling the pull, the draw, of the water meeting the horizon. The feeling of being at the brink of endlessness, the way the vast expanse of water follows a rhythm all its own. Just as we follow the rhythm of the sun, the sea follows the rhythm of its orbiting reflection, the moon. And the syncopation of our interactions—life to life—pulls us to each other, a syncopated dance.

I remember sailing the sound, the sheer wonder of skimming the surface of endless water. The feeling of weightlessness. The intricate communications between waves, wind, wood, and sailcloth. The hand gently laid upon the wheel. I remember my hand on the wheel, feeling the touch of the sea reverberating in my fingertips.

I remember the feeling of sailing the sea without the need of a destination, without the urgency of time, with only an endpoint in the distance to keep the compass aligned.

In the geography of Mark's Gospel thus far, the sea is the center of the labyrinth.

Jesus and his circle spiral around it, to and fro. It draws them back in and propels them away. It brings them to other shores and back again to familiar terrain. It is the mirror of their own souls, endless and adrift, following a rhythm all its own, a syncopated dance.

What is it about this sea, site of storms and miracles?

What is it about the soul, site of doubt and belief?

They were straining at the oars. Jesus has walked the labyrinthine path down the mountain. He is standing at the shore. He is alight with the spark of divinity, its solitude. Jesus is looking at his companions, maybe for minutes, maybe hours upon hours. He observes them work at sail and oar and rudder. He is savoring the last moments of solitude before his own work begins anew. The syncopated pulse of the waves laps his feet, his toes sink into fluid sand.

He is being taken in by the irresistible sea.

Then: he takes the first step. He stands on the surface of the sea, as if on solid ground.

He is lit by moonlight, and his reflection shimmers on the fractured mirror of the sea. He sprints and leaps on its surface. He strides waves and skates smooth alleys of water.

He is a whirling dervish, walking on water.

He is beyond words.

And he would have gone right on by his disciples. He would have kept going if he could. He would have simply met them on the other side of the sea, standing on the opposite shore.

But they see him. And they are screaming.

They are a discordant, shrieking horror, terrorized with fear at the sight of him. And their fear is mirrored in his compassion. *Take heart. It is I. Do not be afraid.* And his compassion swells their courage. They now row quietly in a quiet sea. To see him here is to see what we know and what remains unknown, and to know that we will never know him as fully as he knows us.

The Son of Man rows with them, the pores of his brow glistening with labor.

But his face, dimmed in the night, still grins with his former delight.

In Sweden, ancient labyrinths dot the shoreline of the sea. For reasons we can't quite comprehend, they were built by fishermen nearly one thousand years ago. We conjecture that they were built around legends of life and work at sea. We conjecture that they were built to catch the wicked wind in their center, a plea for good weather at sea. We conjecture that they were built to ward off bad luck, thresholds at the door of the unknown.

Or maybe, just maybe, these Nordic labyrinths were their own kind of map, an atlas of the sea, site of storms and miracles, an atlas of the soul, site of doubt and belief.

The labyrinths in Sweden are known but unknown, perhaps even unknowable.

They mark familiar territory, commonplace, on a Tuesday like any other day.

19

The Number Eleven

AND YOU DO MANY THINGS LIKE THIS. The words whisper in my ear as I do the thing I have now done many times.

It is near the end of day when I enter the churchyard. The day reached its zenith and now descends into the evening chill. As I approach, I meet again the scurrying rabbits, this time two, and I see where they have made their nest, under a shrub beside the church. They skirt along the building wall to keep a safe distance.

I begin my ritual walk slowly in circles. I am in no rush.

卐

Now is a decisive moment in the Gospel (Mk 7:1-13). Scribes from Jerusalem—the center of authority—have gathered around the itinerant rabbi. And the tension bristles the hairs on the back of their necks. They see things that disturb them, that disturb tradition.

Why do your disciples . . . eat with defiled hands?

Jesus bristles. Homeless hands have no place for washing. He looks down at his own open palms, the creases lined with dirt. His hands have touched multitudes of sick and washed them clean. His labor—the inbreaking of the One who holds the cosmos in his own hand—is interrupted by the small-minded legalism of those who hold stones in theirs.

Jesus' jaw stiffens and clenches to a scowl. And the words spew forth, a rapid fire. The prophet speaks a prophet's words. The scribes respond in kind. The argument escalates. After the heated exchange, Jesus utters the indictment, slowly, emphatically.

You abandon the commandment of God and hold to human tradition.

But the word Jesus speaks that we read as *hold* is stronger than that. A better reading: you *seize* human tradition. You *seize* as a master seizes, by violence, force, coercion. And to take tradition by force is to forsake the powerful, creative, healing, liberating Word of God. It is to abandon the living reign of God, the living faith of the dead, for the dead faith of the living.

This is the decisive moment.

I confess: on any given day, I wash my hands often. Before every meal. After entering my home. During breaks at work. It borders on compulsion, this rite of soap and water. As I begin my walk, I remember a few days before, when I had my son wash his hands. And I caught myself wondering whether I was passing my compulsion on to him.

I confront the question of tradition and force, of what I seize and what seizes me.

Even further: Is this labyrinth walk a commandment of God or a human tradition? Is this spiritual discipline, this ritual observance, a lip service or a service of the heart? I am walking this path after supper at Winslow's Home with my wife and son. They have walked home. I remain. Have I abandoned these loves for the sake of my own tradition?

I have no answers to these questions. Except for this: perhaps the fact I am asking the questions at all is an answer in itself. It at least reflects a certain self-awareness. But that is a small comfort.

Perhaps the answer is in the dissonance the questions cause, the heightening tension within, the heart's agitation. Perhaps there is an irresolvable tension between ritual and experience, between discipline and action.

Perhaps the answer is the tension that listens in the silence after the question.

The church labyrinths, of which the medieval labyrinth in Chartres Cathedral is the masterpiece, innovated the design of the labyrinth from seven circuits to eleven. This is what made the labyrinth Christian, the symbolism of the number eleven.

Eleven: one more than the Ten Commandments but one less than the twelve apostles. Simultaneously, it is the number of excessiveness and incompleteness, the excessively incomplete, the incompletely excessive. Eleven: the in-between sign of broken humanity, caught in the force of tradition. Eleven: the symbol of questions without answers.

Eleven: eleven circuits in Chartres for the labyrinth of sin.

I reach the center lost in thought. The rabbits are nowhere to be seen. I pray my ritual prayer. I walk back out of the circle in a trance of half-emptiness, thoughts excessive and incomplete.

As I come round the circuit nearest the sanctuary, my half-empty thoughts are interrupted by sounds of singing.

A choir is singing. And only now do I see gilded light through the sanctuary windows. Only now has the dusking day grown dark enough that I can see it, grown quiet enough to hear it.

And then I remember: I stand in a churchyard on a Wednesday evening in Lent. A church gathers for the discipline of a pilgrimage, even as I walk my own. I walk out of the maze and approach the sanctuary window, to listen close.

But as I walk toward the wall, I stop short.

I am standing face to face with a rabbit. She crouches between me and the wall. We see each other, eye to eye. I am looking into the full circle of her round, dark eye. I lean back to allay her suspicion. I back away and walk around the sanctuary's edge. The singing swells, but it is made brittle by stone. I hear an organ begin to play.

I stand at the entrance to the church. I decide to try the sanctuary doors, to enter in.

I am stopped short again. The door is locked.

The singing quiets.

The questions remain.

20

Between the Lines

YESTERDAY IT WAS DUSK WHEN I reached the labyrinth. Today it is dark. Nine o'clock. The night is cool, but the icy chill is gone. Perhaps now, this last night of March, winter has truly passed.

But I am not holding my breath.

I can read the path of the maze in the dark. But there are points and turns where I look close to make sure I don't mistake mud for brick, or brick for mud. The night requires such concentrated attention, such close reading of the lines, deciphering its secrets.

The labyrinth is meant to be read, even in the dark.

I read between its lines.

The labyrinth creates a curious paradox between what is inside and what is outside. There is no privileged knowledge here. Its entrance is open and free to all. Once I'm inside, it makes of me an insider, tantalizingly close to the center. But then as it turns, it makes of me an outsider again, precariously close to the edge of its world.

And yet whether I am outside or inside, it always leads me to the center. Open and free to all who step into its path.

Or perhaps only because I have already been both outsider and insider, it grants me access to its center. It deconstructs the pretension of the one and the subjugation of the other. All the pilgrims who walk its path walk the same path, regardless of status or station or standing. No one gets special access. All count the same cost of pilgrimage. And the cost is nothing except the willingness to set one foot in front of the other.

Jesus' ferocity over the morning's argument lingers into the afternoon, then into the night (Mk 7:14-23). So he continues to speak, turning to those closer to his heart, speaking more softly now, but still severe.

There is a radical logic to Jesus' words. Radical as in *radix*, to the root. He speaks to the root of things, to the root physiology of existence. *There is nothing outside a person that by going in can defile, but the things that come out are what defile.* Food enters the stomach, but action and behavior arise from the heart.

There is a radical logic to this parable. I read between its lines.

On the surface it retains a stunning simplicity, but beneath the surface it contains an entire code of ethics. This is its labyrinth, that it deconstructs both what is inside and what is outside. *For it is from within, from the human heart, that evil intentions come.* The list that follows is broad enough to indict all humankind.

The paradox is that the heart is the only purely internal organ, fed only by other organs, its blood enclosed in vessels beneath the skin, its electric pulse involuntary. And yet it is only through the heart's internal combustion that the human exhaust of pollution enters the world. Like the cut that opens the spurt of blood into air, the violence of the heart begins in the razor-edge of word and deed meant to cut a wound, one body to another.

And too often, the body that is cut is our own.

It is evening now, dark. He sits in the house in a simple linen tunic as he speaks. His homeless disciples bear only the clothes on their back. They sit round him as they always do. He is the center, and as always, he does not allow them to sit in the same places. They rotate around him in a way that makes of them both outsiders and insiders. No one gets a permanently privileged place. The words of prophets come to the prophet again:

> rend your hearts and not your clothing.
> Return to the LORD, your God,
> for he is gracious and merciful,
> slow to anger, and abounding in steadfast love. (Joel 2:13)

The words that are answers to questions provoke more questions. The disciples ask, and the rabbi answers in turn.

Do you also fail to understand?

He speaks with an urgency and a sharp-edged clarity, cutting to the quick. His words cut marrow from bone, not to wound but to debride the heart, to make it whole. And even if they are not aware of exactly what he is doing, they can feel under their ribs how Jesus is stripping their hearts bare. He is stripping all things bare, to their root. He is laying bare the nature of the world.

This is the radical paradox of the parable, that only in its radical simplicity can it contain the logics of the world and of human action within it.

He speaks until drowsiness overtakes them. Reclining in the circle, they will all soon sleep to rise at the break of dawn. They fall asleep—one by one—hanging on his words.

They will dream in parables.

Before walking away, I turn and behold the labyrinth whole, dark ground streaked with darker lines. In the dark, things are seen and unseen.

In the dark, I am reading the labyrinth, trying to read between its lines.

I behold the labyrinth whole, trying to decipher its secrets.

So much of our life is really its own act of reading, trying to make sense of what we know and what we don't know. Even the act of reading is its own kind of labyrinth. We read the same lines, the same passages, over and over again to get their meaning, to receive new meaning in their old words. We've even made a spiritual practice—the *lectio divina*—

of the labyrinth of reading, reading over and over again the same sacred text, peering into the center of its meaning, reading between its lines.

Standing in the dark, I know that life is sometimes lived in a painful tension between what we see and what we do not see, seeing and un-seeing. I remember reading Annie Dillard. I remember the passage she writes about the minute graces the specialist sees that the nonspecialist misses, and about the striving to see copper pennies hidden in the twisting lines of sycamore trees.

At this moment, I am not a specialist in anything I see around me, at least not that I am aware. But perhaps there is in this naiveté something just as profound, an open secret hidden in between the lines.

21

Secret

THIS IS THE DAY I HAVE BEEN WAITING FOR, longing for. A day for rejoicing in. The Saturday air is clear and clean. The morning is brimming with the aroma of blooming things. The woody stalks of hydrangea are dappled with lime leaves. The first blades of hosta are poking the surface of soil. New mulch arbors the air with the notes of earth. The open spaces seem to crackle with the breaking forth of waking life. This is sabbath: that life lives, moves and has being of its own accord, without force or coercion.

I walk to the churchyard.

The morning is neither cold nor hot. The breeze is cool while the sun is warm. The sanctuary doors are open. From within, a froth of conversation flows over into the street. I sneak past and enter the labyrinth with leisurely steps. My day bears no commitments beyond this one. It will live and move and have being of its own accord. As I wind the path, I can feel my brow tingle with perspiration. But I do not sweat.

It occurs to me that whenever I have walked the labyrinth, I have never looked at a clock. This was not intentional, but nonetheless I take pride in it and commit myself to it for the rest of this pilgrimage. I turn the accident into an intention.

Because there is a kind of timelessness in the labyrinth. This despite the fact that it is not without process or movement, both of which require the passing of time. But it does not require time's measure into seconds, minutes, hours, days, weeks, months, years. It keeps time without marking or division. It keeps time in secrets and paradoxes.

In this sense, the labyrinth acts more like the compass than like the clock. It guides us by telling us where we *are* at any given moment and not where we need to *go*. It doesn't press us into what will be in the next second or minute or hour. It allows for the rest that stands in the liminal moment between the tick and the tock.

By the time I reach the center, my body has cooled. The whispers of wind, unnoticed, have cooled my head. My body has reached equilibrium with the air. I bow my head and see my shadow, pointing like a compass arrow to the northwest. I pray.

Hallowed be thy name.

Hallowed be this ground. Hallowed be these minutes and days, this sabbath of time in between time. Hallowed be the reign of God breaking forth in springtime.

Having crossed the boundaries of abstract legalism, Jesus now crosses the border of a holy geography (Mk 7:24-37). He has chosen again the land of Gentiles, the land of the unchosen.

He is now again a refugee.

He enters the village under the disguise of night, with stealth. He and his companions are sidling single file, their backs against walls. They come upon the house marked for them. He knocks quietly on the door. He wants to remain a secret. They enter in silence, but not unnoticed.

He could not escape notice.

Because, as they say, mothers always know. Mothers always find out. So also with this mother who bangs on the door at dawn. She can hear the hushed froth of conversation within. Pushing through the cracked-open door, she begs at his feet. He knows the word is out. His secret is out.

He sighs. His brow tingles. Somewhere within, in the thin crackle of the air, he can hear the stomping crowd soon to emerge.

But there is nothing in this woman's blood, in her flesh, that is chosen. She is Syrian and she is Greek, an unchosen Gentile.

Jesus beckons her to sit at the table. He will speak to her the way he always now speaks. He speaks to her in parable.

It is not fair to take the children's food and throw it to the dogs.

And that is when it happens. An incredible thing happens.

The woman speaks back.

But that is not the incredible thing.

The woman speaks back in parable, in words with a secret meaning.

Sir, even the dogs under the table eat the children's crumbs.

He is startled, his eyes wide, his mouth open. No man, nor woman, has ever reversed the paradox of parable back upon him. Is he feigning his surprise? Could he have anticipated this? Was it a test? The disciples ask each other, but they do not know.

Neither do we.

All we know is that Jesus sees a faith before him he has never seen, from a woman, from among those unchosen, from the land where he is the refugee.

Somewhere, in a room on the other side of town, a child quiets. Her seizure leaves her. The demon is gone.

Somewhere deep within, Jesus knows it is futile to keep the secret of himself secret.

Nevertheless, he departs and detours. Back to the sea, but along its eastern shore. He stays on the move, a step ahead of the crowd. The disciples are breathless to keep pace. They arrive at the city limits of the Decapolis, but the secret has caught up to them. A crowd awaits.

Jesus sighs again.

They bring forth a man who neither speaks nor hears. He resists their pushing. He shrugs his shoulders before the prophet, as if to acknowledge that he wanted to remain a secret too. Jesus senses a kindred spirit with this man.

He pulls him aside. He pulls him into a marvelous and intimate secrecy. The crowd will not share in this secret. Not even his disciples enter into this house of his presence.

But we are here.

We are the only witnesses to the marvelous secret.

They kneel down in the dirt. Jesus has his back to us, but we can see the man's face over his shoulder. With deep gentleness, we see Jesus touch one ear, then the other, with his hand. We hear Jesus spit in his hand. We see him rub the saliva into salve—healing balm—upon the man's outstretched tongue. We can almost feel it tickle our tongue.

And then he throws his head back and sighs once more.

But this sigh is deeper than the others, as deep as the sea, as deep as the recesses of his own secret being. A sigh nearly too deep for words.

Except for one word. We hear the word but we do not know its meaning.

Eph–pha–tha! he sighs.

Be opened!

And this shall be the first word the man ever hears. *Ephphatha.* Be opened. Because *immediately* his ears are opened. His tongue is loosed. And we know because we hear him talk, and his talk is plain speech. We hear words. Jesus and the man speak to each other in hushed tones, a secret conversation. We hear only the sound of their sentences, as if through the closed door of the next room. We hear the rhythm of words, without their sense. It is a melody all its own.

They delight to share this secret, each to the other. No one else will hear it, not even us. At its heart is a timelessness without the measure of time.

And for one moment Jesus stays where he is, without a thought of where he needs to go.

As Jesus ushers the man back to the crowd, he is smiling, silently. But the man can't stop talking. Like a child whose whole world is opening anew in language, he is a rushing torrent of words. Jesus knows the paradox of his secret: the more he tries to conceal it, the more it is opened up upon the world. *Ephphatha.*

Thus the secret of the reign of God, the direction of its compass. Thus the astonishment of the people, *beyond measure.*

Indeed, this man does everything well.

Upon leaving the labyrinth, I try to steal past the open doors of the sanctuary. I am curious but I do not want to step inside. I feel bashful. I fear the feeling of being caught, my secret discipline revealed. I want to remain hidden, unknown. As I walk past, a man steps to the threshold from inside. He smiles. I smile back. But we do not speak. The secrets of spring are being opened up to glory all around us, and we dare not say a word.

I keep walking. Down the steps, to the sidewalk, down the hill, to the busy street. Across the street, the patio at Winslow's Home is packed with people breaking their fast. I meet them by their scents: maple syrup, oatmeal, bacon. All mixing with the honeyed dogwood blossoms flitting beside me, an intermingling that defies description.

This much I know: any attempt at describing anything of this moment would be too trite. A greeting-card poem can't help but fail to describe the sublime immensity of the world, the way it arises to life in spring, an immensity that opens up in little blossoms, in the tingle of a bead of sweat on the brow.

Perhaps this is why I want to keep this discipline a secret. Perhaps this is why I didn't want to speak to the man at the threshold. I don't want to try to explain what remains a sweet mystery, known and unknown at the same time. Silence seems its only explanation, the hush of the sound of words we cannot understand, the sigh too deep for words.

Eph–pha–tha.

And yet there are these words, this word. I may yet learn to speak its lines.

I walk home in complete silence. This whole world is awake and alive, rinsing itself of the grit and grunge of winter. I want to remain a silent secret within it, not to be hidden, but to absorb all of this waking delight.

22

Cross

THE NEW DAY FORESHADOWS THE MONTHS TO COME. A spring day with summer heat. The thermometer touches 90 degrees Fahrenheit. But the heat is blustered by wind, and by nightfall the wind will bring storms.

Everything about this day seems a foreshadowing of things to come.

I wait to walk the labyrinth until the mellow sun sits low in the western sky. The shadows are long in the churchyard. As I approach, four robins skitter the yard, along with a squirrel. They scatter and fly as I become visible to them. The only trace left of their life is the melody I hear in the trees.

Caesarea Philippi (Mk 8:27-38). The region gives name—Hail Caesar!—to the heavy hand of Rome and empire. Jesus has left behind the crowds and walks alone with his disciples. They walk along the outskirts of towns. With every step, they walk farther north than they have ever walked before.

With the circle of disciples, we stand now at the center of the Gospel, and at the center comes the question. Every act of power, every miracle of healing, has been pressing for its answer. We are pressing for the secret to the question. Its answer is a secret.

Jesus stops and turns in his tracks, facing his followers.

Who do people say that I am?

Echoing in the air, the question seems to come from nowhere and everywhere at once. Finally, he asks it of himself. The disciples have been hanging on every word, waiting for it. Hanging on every word, we have waited for it. And behind the question is the deeper question, the one that cuts to the quick.

Who am I?

Peter answers the only answer left to give, the only one that makes any sense.

Prophet? Rabbi? King?

Peter answers: *Messiah.*

The Christ. The Son of God.

And for once, we circle back to the beginning. The beginning of the good news. Every story has its beginning. Here in the middle, this one begins again.

This is who Jesus is. The Christ. *Messiah.*

Yes, now all that was mystery begins, but only begins, to make sense.

Because Jesus answers Peter's answer with words more strange. This is what will happen to the Christ: *the Son of Man must undergo great suffering . . . be rejected . . . be killed, and after three days rise again.* The words are open and plain enough, but their meaning is mystery and doom. Standing at the center of the Gospel, the answer to the question only raises more questions.

The disciples stand before him dumbfounded.

It will be a long time before the name is spoken again. They dare not speak it. The name of Christ, revealed, recedes into secrecy once again.

Soon, very soon, the circle of disciples is encircled by crowds. At the center of the Gospel of Mark stands its central figure, teaching them all. Only now, under the weight of a time grown sad, he speaks plainly to them in words they cannot understand, words known but unknowable, a labyrinth of words.

If any want to become my followers, let them deny themselves and take up their cross and follow me.

He has brought his circle within a circle to its northernmost point to bid them bear something they did not know they had, something they do not want, something they sought their whole life to avoid.

A cross. Their cross. The symbol of tyranny, torture, pain, violence, oppression, death. The sign of Caesar. All amazement is now gone. Only dread remains.

For those who want to save their life will lose it.

Those who lose their life for my sake . . . will save it.

Life and death. Loss and gain. The words are plain, but their meaning a mystery. Even as the question is answered, much remains a mystery. It will take a lifetime to learn.

The disciples are not so naive as before, and in that they have gained. To lose our illusions is to gain the truth. To lose the life they had is to gain the life they now live. This is the paradox of the way they are walking, a lifetime to learn.

To know the answer to Jesus' question is to raise the question of their own identity, my own identity. Who am I? I feel like the last to know. I must become last to know.

I must lose life to gain it.

It will take a lifetime to learn.

From within the crowd, Jesus turns his face from the north. His feet swivel his body, and he turns to the south. His next step will turn him from north to south. His feet will mark the turn of the arc in the path.

Jesus and his disciples will never again take a step north. Hidden in the south's horizon is the city, the holy city, where every illusion will be left behind.

The most ancient of labyrinths is drawn first by drawing a cross. To draw the cross is the first step in drawing the circling path. The cross is the first mark to make the circle of the square, connecting its arms to the dots between them. The arcs of the path open and blossom around it like petals to the flower.

And yet the labyrinth's cross is not its center. The cross is *in* the path, embedded in its way. The cross is not its center. It is the path *to* the center. I draw this cross, I bear this cross, to reach the center of the maze. Even as the path is plain, its center remains mysteriously unknown, empty, a secret.

As I walk the maze, I think of tragic figures. Daedalus. Oedipus. Hamlet. Lear. Haunting words emerge from the recesses of memory. Jesus of Nazareth is taking upon himself the secret heroism of tragedy. The vortex of his being is pulling him inexorably to tragedy's end. He sees the long foreshadows. He foresees how the spiral of this path is swirling swiftly to its center.

Tragic lines emerge from memory.

The weight of this sad time we must obey;
Speak what we feel, not what we ought to say.
The oldest hath borne most: we that are young
Shall never see so much, nor live so long.

The words belong to the weak and helpless Albany, King Lear's lifeless body at his feet. But the final line is Shakespeare's alone, never spoken on the stage:

Exeunt, with a death march.

Such is the inevitable spiral of tragedy, inwardly turning then outward again.

A death march.

In the last quadrant of the labyrinth, the path moves back and forth like a funnel, each curve bending closer and quicker toward the center. It pulls me inescapably to the center, gaining whirlpool speed. Something within me recoils to reach the center, to know the knowledge that comes of time made tragic.

Nevertheless, I stand at the center. And I pray.

Thy will be done.

I pray. Then I exit. But I exit by walking a straight line cut through the maze, stepping over the arced lines of the circuits, straightaway out of the labyrinth, straight home. My long shadow foreshadows me home.

This day, I cannot bear to unwind the path again, to circle back around this deathly knowledge, this path made of a cross. I cannot bear it.

The tragic question shadows my steps.

Who am I?

It will take a lifetime to learn. I fear it will require a death to know.

I straightaway exit, the steps their own death march.

part five

Practicing the Everyday

It is funny, and often frustrating, how one moment of epiphany catapults us so quickly back into the humdrum of everyday existence, how its ecstatic thrill dissolves so quickly into the monotony of everyday routine.

I mention it because I can't help but feel like I am walking in circles, over and over again.

My life in circles.

This path in circles.

I feel like I am walking in circles. In walking this labyrinth, in this season in between the seasons, even in writing these words, I feel like I am walking in circles. Around and around, over the same things, the same thoughts, the same ground again and again, seeming to never get anywhere.

I would not blame you if the same thought had crossed your mind, that we are circling the same place over and over again.

But now the irony of it hits me:

This is what the labyrinth is. Literally, figuratively, spiritually. This is what the labyrinth is, and this is what the labyrinth is for: walking in circles, around and around, over the same ground, again and again.

I feel like I am walking in circles because I *am* walking in circles.

And isn't this what life is like sometimes: walking in circles, around and around the same ground? We get caught in the midst of our day-by-day routines—days, weeks, months, years—and it seems we have gone nowhere but right back to where we started.

But here lies the beauty in the irony of the labyrinth. Rather than deny the reality of the routine, it lifts it up to light. Rather than defy the menial repetitions of life, it makes of them a discipline. Rather than begrudge the circling around and around, it opens my life to the ways the world can change with just one step. One step, one turn, one twist in the path changes the whole perspective of the journey, breaking open the beauty of what is new in what had been, one step prior, so mundane.

In this sense, walking the labyrinth is not a practice for making "progress" per se, or even about reaching a certain destination. It is a practice for seeing and perceiving everyday routines, habits, ad infinitum, in a new kind of light. It flies in the face of the assumption that spirituality is only about constant progression, because it reminds us that the spiritual life is just as often about being able to stand still amid everyone else's mad dash for greener grass.

In the middle of these forty days, this is what the labyrinth is teaching me, again.

Perhaps this is the spirituality at the heart of the labyrinth: to open a life to the newness of life that we can find only when we are standing still for a moment, to let go of the notion that we can find our purpose only when we have gone from whatever is *here* to whatever we think we can find over *there*. Perhaps the spirituality of the labyrinth is rooted in the awareness that the greener grass is the grass under our feet, the grass that will lift once again when we lift our foot to take the next step.

Perhaps this is what the apostle Paul means when he speaks of *the secret of being content* (Phil 4:12). Yes, the *secret* of contentment, hidden in emptiness.

There is this remarkable empathy to the labyrinth. If the labyrinth is a symbol of life, its circuits mimic the tortuous circles our lives often take. But it circles us around the center one step more. In its circuitous rhythm, it makes of our mundane lives a dance all its own. In its singular path to the same center, it makes a pilgrimage all its own. It makes a pilgrimage of walking in circles, staying in place.

Every step is the same. But every walk is different.

More to the point, the labyrinth lifts us to the awareness that when the rest of the world is spinning ever more swiftly in circles, often the only progress is to stand still. As a matter of fact, the labyrinth, all its ways leading to the center, deconstructs our innumerable myths of progress, our ideas that life can become better only when we are ascending a straight line from *here* to *there*, always looking for the advantage that will get us one more rung up the ladder, one more step ahead of the other.

Perhaps the labyrinth is teaching me that the only way to truly run in circles is to think that I should be anywhere else than right *here*, right *now*, in the secret promise of this present moment, a promise given to me—pure gift—if I would only have eyes to see and ears to hear.

Of course, it strikes me as more than coincidence that I write all this the morning after I reread Jorge Luis Borges's short story "The Gospel According to Mark." We call it a short story, but it reads more like a parable. It tells the story of Baltasar Espinosa, an Argentinian medical student who decides to spend the summer of 1928 on his cousin's countryside ranch. While his cousin is away, a flood comes and quickly strands him there alone, completely isolated except for the Gutres, a family of illiterate ranch hands who do the ranch's menial everyday work. As the flood rises, Baltasar invites the three of them into the large farmhouse, to give them better shelter and to ward off his own loneliness. And this becomes their daily evening routine, after dinner: he reads to them from the family Bible he finds among the few books on the shelf.

He starts, at all places, with the Gospel According to Mark.

And then, a strange thing happens. When they get to the end of the Gospel of Mark, Baltasar intends to move on to another book. But the Gutres beg him to read the same story again. Like little children listening to the same bedtime story over and again, they ask him to go back to the beginning and reread the Gospel of Mark.

So Baltasar goes back to the beginning and reads it again, a second time. And the feeling the reader gets reading Borges's parable is that if the story didn't shift here, Baltasar would still be reading the Gospel of Mark to the Gutres, over and over the same ground, into all eternity.

That's not how Borges's story ends, of course, but I think this little image in the middle of it strikes at something profound. Jorge Luis Borges knew what I am discovering. The Gospel of Mark walks mysteriously in circles too. Even its geography walks in circles: here, in and around Galilee, then across the sea, only to return to Galilee to spiral again the sea. For all its speed, Mark walks in circles around and toward a secret center, hidden and empty.

What is it about the Gospel of Mark? It is a labyrinth, as mysterious as the parables buried like seeds within it. And yet it is *the beginning of the good news*, irresistibly drawing us in and circling us around, turning over the same ground, making it holy.

When we get down to it, Mark shares this profundity with the labyrinth as a spiritual practice. Many spiritual practices want to get you from *here* to *there*. They have the sense of a straight-line pilgrimage of progress. But the labyrinth opens our way to the *there* that is already *here*, the *here* already *there*. The labyrinth is the spiritual practice of the everyday, the staying in place, the standing still. Turning over the same ground, tilling it with its curves, it makes it holy.

Every life goes through its own struggle or pain, crisis or ordeal, no doubt about that. But most days when people ask me how I'm doing, I respond with familiar words: *Can't complain*. And most of the time, I more or less mean it.

And let's be honest. In our heart of hearts, we want most of our life to go like that. Most of us don't want to live from crisis to crisis, from pain to pain. We try to find, each in our own way, a kind of level normalcy, an even keel to keep afloat.

I began walking the labyrinth out of simple curiosity. It seemed like a good thing to do. But underneath the curiosity was the nagging sense that life can too easily become a meaningless repetition of routines, and the familiar words become a mask hidden in a cliché.

Can't complain.

I'm fine. How about you?

This too is its own kind of labyrinth, a maze of familiarity, a maze of routine, walking the same path day in and day out, a mindless habit of one day to the next.

In this sense, the labyrinth opens us to the double-entendre of anything we would call a *practice*. We use the word *practice* to refer to our actions and customs, to how we perform an act, to what happens in the "real world." This is *practice* as opposed to *theory*. But we also use the word to refer to our rehearsals of what we hope to do in everyday life, to how we prepare for an event, to those drills we repeat over and over again to produce the skill we need to live. This is the *practice* as opposed to the *game*.

Both uses, both meanings, of the word are profoundly and utterly true.

But we tend to demean the sense of practice as rehearsal. It takes second place to the game, to the "real world," often because it can feel so boring, so redundant. Like walking in circles. Yet in actuality, most of our life is a rehearsal for what we could never achieve on our own. Every day we practice our life in the hope of a perfect day. We rehearse for it. We never reach it, of course. Every day has its inevitable failures, its brokenness, its pain. But we go to sleep and awake again to a new day, another rehearsal, until we reach the day that will interrupt our everyday, the day the Scriptures call *the day of the Lord*. The perfect day. We practice every day to live into that fullness, to see it breaking into our everyday, interrupting it with the surprise, the grace, the mystery of God.

We practice it—walking the labyrinth—to find the *presence* in time, ordinary time. In it, the rhythm of walking summons the sacred within the everyday, the holy within every day.

This becomes the muscle memory of faith. We practice it so that when failure and adversity and pain inevitably arise, we can lean on what we have practiced most repeatedly, on the life we have rehearsed with our trust, over and over again.

But the stunning reality is that as I practice the everyday—walking this labyrinth of life—I am finding how it makes me more and more attentive to details. To the way the bark wrinkles the branch like a furrowed brow. To the timbre and tone of a voice. To the affectionate wiggle of a little finger.

The call of the labyrinth is to live each day on its own terms, in the way each day calls us to live it, each day its own gift of life made new. This is what it means to say, *This is the day that the* LORD *has made,* and to rejoice in it, this day made and given by an ever-giving Creator, given for rejoicing.

Every day simultaneously the same and different.

Every day its own labyrinth of beautiful design.

And it is only when I become attentive to the details, attentive to and aware of how they bring me to the threshold of rejoicing, that I grow in the unfathomable skill of what it means to love.

23

Transfigured

I ARRIVE AT THE LABYRINTH TWO HOURS AFTER DUSK. The night is clear, but the moon has not yet risen. A handful of stars speckle the navy-blue dome, smooth as silk. I have found that I like to take my walk after dark. The starry night is a painting by van Gogh, swirling stars in inky sky, thin spike of a church steeple, the city lying below. I stand in it, a pink-fleshy streak of pigment amid midnight blue dappled with gray.

In the luminous dark, the labyrinthine path is illuminated in a kind of reverse light, a photonegative, the brick path outlined in heavy shadow, the grass the color of ash.

The night is its own secret. And I can walk as a secret in the night.

The labyrinth is a sign of secrets, hidden in the night.

In the fifteenth century, the Italian Robertus Valturius inscribed a flag standard on parchment, on which was drawn a labyrinth. The parchment was the page of a military manual, *De re militari.* The labyrinth was the sign that a military commander's plans must remain as much a secret as the center of the circuits of a labyrinth remain hidden. Thereafter, the labyrinth became an emblem, sewn to flags, embroidered on the chest, for Italian princes and generals of the secrecy of their intentions. The labyrinth embroidered on the shirt covered the prince's heart, shrouding the heart's plans in secrecy.

The labyrinth is a sign of unseen secrets made in the night, plans and plots and intentions.

The labyrinth is a sign of the unseen heart, all its secrets.

But this night, the labyrinth is transfigured in night light. I walk the secret of its mystery in tortuous circuits, the chambers of a heart.

What is it to have a thing, a life, transfigured before our eyes, to have its heart embroidered with light? What is it to be transfigured? For Jesus of Nazareth, it is to have the luminosity of his being shine forth, no longer a secret, but still a mystery in light.

It is to have the identity of his life—the luminous identity of all life—made sublime.

It is to see the Christ of Jesus.

It is to witness the truth of life in a way beyond description, beyond words. It is life transcending and transcendent, a mystery beyond mysteries, a life beyond life. He is as sublime as the sea, more dazzling than the sea of stars.

His clothes became dazzling white, whiter than anyone in the world could bleach them (Mk 9:3 NIV).

To witness it is to be turned speechless at the truth within the truth of life. To be transfigured is to have life revealed face to face, beyond the secret emblems of its description.

I pray with my head lifted to the heavens. I fix my eye upon one star. I have no idea how far this particular sun is from earth, but I know its light has spent years, centuries, traveling to earth, to my sight.

Could it have been that its light first ignited in the day of this man from Nazareth? Could it have sparked its genesis in the time of the Christ? Two thousand years to touch earth, to kiss my eye.

Its flickering light becomes sublime. A star is transfigured amid the darkness of night.

For the three disciples, coming down the mountain is as painstaking as the ascent (Mk 9:2-10 NIV). Their muscled legs brace against the steep face of the hill to stay their bodies from the fall. The descent is as slow and rigorous as the climb was breathless and grueling. Yet in between breaths, there is word and wonder enough to speak. They will indeed obey. They will keep the secret of this mountain. They will not cross the threshold to try to describe vainly what is indescribable.

The sky above them is clear, smooth as silk, and it is turning to night. The first stars begin to flicker alive. The moon has not yet risen.

They will keep the secret of this mountain, even as it gives rise to irresistible questions.

What does it mean? What does it mean?

The wonder of their words is the beginning of the rest of the journey. He is—in all his rediscovered plainness along the plain: plain face, plain ground, plain linen—walking ahead of them, farther ahead with each step. Thin dust already embroiders his back, covers his heart, with a shadow of earth.

What does it mean? What does it mean, this *rising from the dead*?

24

Facing Failure

I ARRIVE AT THE LABYRINTH AFTER WORK, at the threshold again between work and rest. The coolness of spring is a calm solace in the midst of rushing cars. A squirrel scatters once again at my presence.

Does the squirrel not remember me?

I wonder once more: Am I the only human being who walks this path?

Life returns to the same ground, the plain (Mk 9:14-29). As Jesus and the three approach the disciples who had remained behind, the heat of an argument—violent conflict of words—reaches their ears before they can see from where it arises. The remnant of disciples is surrounded. Teachers of the law surround them. The crowd surrounds them. They are being outwitted. Violence lurks along the tortuous edges of the crowd.

Jesus stops for a moment, still on the way to the circling mob. He groans, a low, quiet growl. The sound of it sends a thin tremor through the air. The crowd awakes to it, as if awakened from slumber. Wild, they rush toward him. He braces himself against them. The three are lost in the rush.

What are you arguing about? He speaks quietly but with authority.

A child is brought forward. Violence lurks upon his tortuous edges. *Immediately*, he is seized by violence, convulsing, roiling in the dust, foaming at the mouth. Jesus speaks to the boy's father, the one and only peaceable voice in the midst of violence. He asks the calm questions of a physician. *How long has this been happening?* All about him is a convulsion of helplessness and failure.

The day's work has me thinking about failure. I will confess that some days I walk this path halfheartedly, only for the routine of it.

But not today.

The spring air is too intoxicating. The grass is beginning, slowly, to surrender itself to new green. Bowed blades are beginning to lift.

The day's work had for the first time returned me to a place of past failure, the place where I was laid off from work years before. I faced failure, even if it was without fault, the failure of circumstances beyond my control. I was at peace to go there, and what welled up in me was no longer anger nor bitterness nor resentment but memory, a circumspect nostalgia. These wounds have healed, a leathered scar. I am at the threshold of a peace not wholly unexpected.

Nevertheless, I am acutely aware that to walk this path is to walk a way made of crosses, on a bed of lifting nails turning green.

To face failure is to face the past convulsing in the dust. I must bear mine as a cross to the center. I plainly face failure again, face the past, face reality, on the same ground, the plain, with no illusions.

I am discovering that the beginning of the bearing up of one's cross is in facing failure.

I pray there the prayer taught to failures.

I make the sign of the cross. I move my hand from forehead to belly button to left shoulder to right shoulder, the hand then left to rest on my heart.

The heart is twice crossed over.

This labyrinth is a path for those who know failure: no cost for admission, no wrong decisions to make, only to follow the direction of the one path.

The labyrinth is where failure surrenders to memory surrenders to hope.

As I walk the way of exit, the seasoned smell of steaks grilling perks my nose. My mouth waters. I am hungry. I walk to return to the place where I am received with open arms, without fail. I walk to my car to return home. I wait for two minutes to be able to turn left onto the speeding street.

The radio speaks once again of global joblessness, thousands upon thousands, the failure of economy.

I cross the threshold and the house is empty. I wait and wait for my loves to return.

The beginning of the bearing up of one's cross is in facing failure.

The cross is failure.

The father's voice bespeaks failure. *I asked your disciples to cast it out, but they could not.* Jesus' voice pronounces failure in slow syllables. *How much longer? How much longer?* Even their belief is halfhearted with failure: *If you are able.*

A courteous belief masks deeper despair.

Jesus groans again, louder. *If you are able?* His tone is acid. A quick, solitary snicker within the crowd turns to utter silence.

Then the cry echoes out, high then low, among the cracks of rocks along the plain, the cracks in its rocky labyrinthine path.

I believe!

Help my unbelief!

The voice cracks high then low with the honesty of failure. The voice's body slumps to its knees. The first step in the bearing of one's cross is the facing of failure, staring it down face to face. The father is face down in the dust. His face is veiled in dust.

Only now does he hear the silence. The loud lunatic noise has ceased. He believes for a moment that sweet death has ceased his boy's suffering. The father looks up to see.

Jesus has laid his hand on the boy's shoulder. The father looks up to see him, the boy's head tilted to the side, resting in the rabbi's side.

The boy is exhausted, his face encrusted with dust. But he stands alive. And on his face grins the quiet smile that turns failure into memory into hope into the labyrinth of his father's heart.

The father's heart has never ached so deeply to embrace his child.

And only now, as I sit in the labyrinth of an empty house, does the detail strike me.

I too am the father of a son. And try as hard as I might, I know this father's failure. So often I feel I have failed my own son, the little failures of everyday living. *Forgive us our trespasses.* I am the father, on my knees before the rabbi from Nazareth.

I believe. Help my unbelief.

Never has my heart ached so deeply to embrace my child.

25

Safe at Home

THE AIR IS STILL BUT FRAGRANT. It is noontime, after a lunch at home, comfort food, away from work. Overnight, bare trees were dotted with green freckles. Overnight, green freckles burst forth into little leaves.

We have entered again into the childhood of the earth.

At home, I watch the baseball game. In the car, I listen to it on the radio. It is a perfect day for baseball: clear, bright, crisply warm.

The baseball diamond is its own kind of labyrinth. A single path always leading to home plate. From the batter's box, around the bases until safe at home, a sprint around the same ground, over and again. Baseball is a team sport concentrated on a solitary journey. In its own vernacular, the journey is a *run*, a race run in circles around the squared diamond, base to base until safe at home.

The game of baseball is its own kind of labyrinth. At its center is the mystery of childhood, the labyrinth of a game that can be practiced but never fully mastered, where success is more often defined by failure, the difficult simplicity of trying to hit a round ball with a round bat squarely.

I walk the labyrinth into the mystery of a game, memories as deep as childhood. I walk and my mind's eye flickers through my memories.

Playing catch.

Learning how to throw a curveball.

Rolling the curveball off my fingers, watching it dive through air.

I walk into the labyrinth into the memory of a game, the mystery of childhood.

Secretly, they enter again into Galilee (Mk 9:30-37). It has been a long journey circling back into familiar towns, places where their accent is hidden, where they know they can hide, unknown and untroubled. Nevertheless, they are troubled. The whispers among the Twelve begin to bubble up into commotion.

The trouble arises from his teaching, troubling words.

The Son of Man is to be betrayed into human hands, and they will kill him, and three days after being killed, he will rise again.

This is now the second time that Jesus speaks of these things, this suffering, this death, these three days. The mysterious ambiguity of plain words spoken unplainly gives rise to deep fear. So the disciples turn their trouble into denial, to questions they think they can answer.

Who is the greatest?

They turn again to rank and station, greatest and least, the old hierarchies of a familiar place. Surely here—safe at home—they can become great again.

Except again he turns the question over into paradox.

Whoever wants to be first must be last of all. A paradox again. First last. Last first. And even now familiar things are made strange. Paradoxes abound in a single line.

The puzzle of a line by Wordsworth echoes in my mind.

The Child is father of the Man.

And so the child stands before them, their father.

The second step in the bearing of one's cross is the being made last, the servanthood of all. The bearing of one's cross is the welcoming of children, the recognizing of the One who shines through the child's face. The disciples are being taught by the child, and by the One who has taken the child in his arms.

Only a little of it do they understand.

Perhaps the best they can do is to understand that they don't understand, to know that they do not know.

The labyrinth is its own paradox, a game of mystery. Throughout history, labyrinths have been the gadgets of games. The learning puzzles of Comenius. The musical labyrinths of Bach. The crossword mazes in my grandmother's paperback books. The wooden box you tilt up, then down, to roll the pellet into the center.

Even a game of hopscotch. Some have linked its history to the ancient dance of the labyrinth.

The labyrinth is a game made of mystery, played by children.

At the center of the labyrinth, I am the child again. Safe at home. As I walk out of the labyrinth, it is as if I am unraveling all the knotty accretions of adulthood, unraveling myself back to childhood.

When I reach the sidewalk, a mother comes out of the door of the church's daycare building. Her toddler bursts forth from behind her. I stand in the childhood of the seasons, amid children.

I am the child again. And this child is my father.

Of course, this is a twist of what Jesus means. *Whoever welcomes one such child*. He does not mean us to become children again. He means us to be the hospitality of children, to welcome them in our arms.

Whoever welcomes one such child in my name welcomes me.

He is the child in our midst. And to welcome this child is to welcome the child's father as well. In the welcome is the communion, a hospitality blessed with grace.

What is it about Jesus that makes him like a child? What is it about children that makes them like Jesus?

I know I do not know. But I think I have seen it in the wild curls of my own child's hair. His unadulterated giggle. His brown eyes, their crystalline wonder.

Jesus is welcomed in the child welcomed by me.

26

In Bloom

OVERNIGHT, SPRING HAS GROWN another surprise. I arrive at the labyrinth to its surprise.

The labyrinth is in bloom.

Overnight, the teaching of the Twelve continues (Mk 9:38-50 NIV). And only now, in the closeness that will embody this latter part of the journey, personalities begin to emerge. They are no longer simply a blurry circle of skin and blood and bone.

We have already heard Peter speak, words sometimes sublime, sometimes foolhardy, sometimes both at once.

John now speaks. He is earnest, cautious, concerned. Where Peter speaks with a singular audacity, John speaks with the tone of one delegated by others. He is giving voice to the earnest concern of them all. None of the others have asked it of him, but they nod as he speaks. He speaks as an advocate, and his words distill their common concern into common clarity. *We told him to stop, because he was not one of us.*

Jesus' words too have been distilled in other ways, at other times, by other people. Some have even claimed his advocacy. If you are not with me, you are against me. The enemy of your enemy is your friend. Either you are for us, or you are against us. Or so goes the cliché.

This is the law of the excluded middle, a stark and severe logic. Either X or not X. No middle ground.

But try as they might, the clichés can't capture the truth. The truth of it is lost. The law of the excluded middle is the law of exclusion, the zero-sum logic of targeting enemies, of forcing bystanders to become allies or foes, the logic of polarization.

The truth is lost in the suspicion.

Whoever is not against us is for us.

Jesus' proverb uses the same words but turns them over again. Their logic is reversed. *Do not stop him. Whoever is not against is for us.* Jesus speaks the words with his arms still embracing, still lifting up, the little child. The child's weight does not grow heavy in his arms. The child's body reclines on the rabbi's chest. The child's round head nuzzles under his chin.

This law, as Jesus speaks it, is the logic of the included middle.

It starts not with an enemy but with an embrace. Of its own, it will not require an enemy. The generosity of his logic sparks as a revelation in the disciples' minds. His voice bespeaks a deeper insight into the world, of the life that flows as an undertow beneath the competing orders of the world. The reign of God undercuts the false dichotomies of the zero-sum game. It refuses to practice this game, the violence in conflict.

Jesus takes his logic one step further.

If any of you put a stumbling block before one of these little ones (NRSV). Jesus lowers his voice to a whisper of stern authority, but the child barely stirs. The child has fallen asleep to the steady beat of his heart, the deep vibrato of his voice.

After all, it is the little ones who will always get caught in the middle. And it is better to exclude a part of our very selves, to exclude the part of ourselves that excludes, than to cut off a life from the life of God.

As the Twelve sit round him, Jesus' words, resolute but tender, make of each one of them a little one. They sit before him as little children, nestled in his embrace.

Intertwined in the grass of the labyrinth, a field of little clover weeds has blossomed purple. Each green string has burst into a flower of five purple petals. They scatter across the circles of brick and grass like salt over food. Weeds are the salt of the ground. They blossom like fire.

I walk the labyrinth admiring weeds as if they were flowers. There is a coolness in the air, like a cup of cool water. The breeze slakes my cheek. At the bottom of the yard, beside the busy street, a man hammers a sign near the front of the church. Steel smacking steel, stakes drive into the earth. The sign is an invitation to the time called Holy Week. It states the schedule of the church's services and their times: Thursday, Friday, Saturday, Sunday.

It foreshadows the sacredness of time, a week made holy by events that the Gospel of Mark has already foreshadowed.

When I reach the labyrinth's center, I reach a conscious decision. I decide to walk as if one leg has been excluded. I will walk the path out of the labyrinth in half-strides, with only one leg stepping forward. My left foot takes the first step. My right foot follows and steps only so far as my left foot has already taken me. Then the left strides one step forward again, the right to follow behind.

I walk as if a part of me has been cut off.

I walk as if one leg has been cut off, a part of me excluded. The walking—half-walking—is slow, deliberate, strenuous. When I lengthen my stride it goes slower still.

I am discovering a paradox of walking, how it can grow slow, then slower still.

The half-walking narrows my concentration to a point and with a rhythm. I feel the details of muscle working with bone. My walking becomes a sort of slow dance, a tortuous two-step turning and turning around a dance floor. This dance has no caper, no flourish. But it is its own kind of slow ballet, slow, then slower still.

Everyone will be salted with fire.

Suffering is fire. Pain is fire. Life is fire. Love is fire.

The Spirit is fire.

We are salted by all these things. Like meat seasoned by the char of an open flame, we are salted by fire. We are salted by life concentrated to a point, with a rhythm. The secret is to be salted without being destroyed, to suffer without being destroyed, to love without being destroyed.

How to know the difference when we feel the heat of the flame? *Be at peace with each other,* Jesus says. Conflict is the fire that destroys. Keep peace within your own soul. Keep peace with the little ones all around you.

Peace is the cup of cold water in the midst of fire.

Walking out of the labyrinth, I begin to feel my right hip burn. The muscles of my left leg begin to ache. I walk a way my body has not practiced, strange movements of muscle and bone.

My muscles singe with salt.

My bones are seasoned with fire.

In a field of flowering weeds, I am learning a new way to walk, a new way to lean into trust. The way is slow, slower still. A rhythm all its own.

27

Child's Play

THERE IS A CHILDLIKE DELIGHT IN THIS SPRING DAY. The kind of day school recesses were made for. A day college students skip class for.

As I sit in my office, my love takes my son to the city's botanical garden. To play. This is her day off. Tonight I will hear Mahler's Symphony no. 2 with a friend at the city's best concert hall. The Resurrection Symphony. A night for a different kind of playing. In playing, the life of dreary things is brought back to life. In a sunny spring, life is brought back into lives near dead.

Resurrection is the virtuosity we discover in our playing and our practice of playing.

The blossoming tree at the bottom of the churchyard is already losing its petals, loosening them to fall to the ground. A pool of white streaked purple and pink deepens on the ground around it, at its roots. A dog I cannot see yips and barks from across the street.

I begin to walk the path of circles.

Without thinking, and for no apparent reason, I begin to count my steps.

To see him playing with the children, blessing them, bearing them up in his arms, the disciples are embarrassed with envy (Mk 10:2-16). A little one is climbing up his shoulder. The little one exclaims, with sheer joy, that he is climbing rabbi mountain.

Jesus is laughing.

They have never heard him laugh with such ruckus. He is tickled with glee. *Whoever does not receive the kingdom of God as a little child will never enter it.* He says it as he giggles.

They are watching the reign of God resurrect a joyful ruckus before them. This joy is its reward. Each disciple wishes to be a child again, to rush the rabbi and tumble into his arms, to enter into this joy. They envy the children.

Jesus sits before them, laughing with the mystery of a child's joy.

Let the little children come. Do not stop them. Jesus is breaking new life into dead lives, broken lives. No one will be held back. Jesus' will is equal to his love. Nothing will be held back.

One. Two. Three. Four . . . I am counting my steps to the center of the labyrinth.

I am playing a game a child would play. I number the steps out loud. As I count, my eyes focus on my feet. I am oblivious to the path. My feet must know the path well. They turn of their own accord in the right places.

My steps slow to keep pace as the numbers I speak slowly lengthen.

Three hundred twenty-two. Three hundred twenty-three. Three hundred twenty-four. Three hundred twenty-five.

My next step touches the center. I take 326 steps to walk the labyrinth. Three times two equals six. I say it out loud. A simple mnemonic to remember the number until I can write it down. Another child's game, a trick for memory.

I wonder. Perhaps no one else will walk this number of steps to walk this labyrinth. Perhaps I will never walk this number of steps to reach the center again. The length of each stride, the turn of each corner, each walk—even over the same ground—can never be the same. The path may be the same, but the steps are always different.

The paradox turns over once again, turns over into a game. My wonder is simple and childlike. This is the game children play.

I hurry my step, circling back through the path to the exit. I do not count my steps. I am hurrying home to my wife and my son. The sun is still up. I want to play whatever games are left to this day to play.

I jog downhill and make a shortcut through the pool of white streaked purple and pink. Even in my hurry I feel the shade of the tree, how the death of the short-lived blossoms has given way to the branches' broader leaves.

28

Marathon

THE HEAT OF A NEW DAY RISES again to a pretense of summer, but with a wind that keeps it from scorching. I wait until the cool of evening to make my walk. Riding on the wind, clouds sail across the sky, the promise of a storm. A single droplet cools a speck of my forearm.

In the air, I can sense that tomorrow will return to cool.

The day is quieting. My muscles ache from yesterday's work: back, legs, shoulders, arms. I laid sod in the front of our home, where an old pin oak tree used to stand. It was chopped down last fall, as it stood dying. Eighty years of life now gone. And if the sod takes hold, it will be as if the tree was never there.

I stand on the sidewalk now, looking at what is no longer there, looking at what now covers over its absence.

Absences are always invisible, the nonexistence within existence. If we weren't there to behold it before—whatever it is—we won't be able to see its absence when it is gone.

What of my life is absence? What is it that I lack? Do I remember it now that it is absent?

Whatever it is, do I remember enough to feel its absence?

There are these holes in the human heart. In their absences, we can only know to seek what we do not know.

I walk the labyrinth to seek after the absence in the human heart, its empty center.

The day is quieting. I walk from the house to the street that borders the church. I wait to cross the street and enter the churchyard. I remember that just a few hours before—this morning—marathon runners ran along this street. Now the street is nearly empty, absent.

If I had not seen the runners this morning, I would have no idea the marathon had taken place. Except that a remnant of the race remains in the churchyard, a sign with flags.

GO GO GO!
Marathoners
Run the good race!

The race I now walk will not be nearly as long, but I have been walking it for days before they started. And will for days still to come.

I wonder: Could the marathon runners feel my absence as I now feel theirs?

It is only after I reach an outer semicircle of the path that I notice in the half-light that the rabbit is again with me. The rabbit watches me but does not run away. I take a small comfort in knowing that I am not walking alone. It is not all absence around me.

As I walk the ground, it has become quiet enough, still enough, that I can hear my footfalls hush the grass.

Jesus wastes no time getting out of town, back to the empty road (Mk 10:17-22 NIV). His disciples scramble to keep pace. Jesus and the disciples have entered Judea, the place of holy places. There can be little mistaking now. They are on the way to Jerusalem. The city. Holy ground. The silhouetted outline of its buildings looms on the horizon, like the little crags of a mountain in the distance.

Their nervousness grows as they take each step closer to the holy city.

They have walked half the morning along the empty road when a solitary figure, breathlessly running, finally catches up. He is sweating and winded. He falls to his knees, half of it a pledge of devotion, the other half a collapse from the marathon of a sprint. In between massive gulps of air, he spits out his question. It is the whole reason he has come to this one moment in the whole history of his life. His whole life seems an absence except for this one moment.

Good Teacher, what must I do to inherit eternal life?

The immediate answer questions the question. *Why do you call me good?*

The man confesses that he has kept every commandment in its entirety, his entire life.

The teacher snorts. Whether the noise is in earnest or irony the disciples do not know. But the second answer raises the stakes of the question.

One thing you lack.

This one absence will bring the man to his knees again. Though his breath is steadying, he is still gasping for air. And it is only now that the disciples see the rich weave of his tunic. For a long time, it would seem, the man has not lacked for anything at all.

The stakes are raised again, higher than ever before.

The rejection the man faces is twofold. He faces the self-rejection of his own identity, the renunciation of all he has inherited in this world to inherit the life that transcends it. And he faces the rejection of the Son of Man, the renunciation into a new way of life, a new way of being.

This second rejection is harder than the first.

The man's breath returns to an even measure. In one fleeting moment, the whole history of his life comes down to this.

The man's face fell.

He cannot bear the thought of the absence of what he now possesses.

The gravity of the thought pulls all the flesh of his face down to a frown. The sadness wells up on his face like beads of sweat. He has run every step of this marathon except this last step. Despite the fact that his heart is throbbing to leap into joy to follow this man, he swallows hard and turns. He swallows again and takes one last deep breath. He begins a long, slow walk home.

It will be nightfall before he reaches the threshold of the door, the lap of luxury.

When he walks in, he will behold again what his house holds, what he could not yet reject. And everything will strike his eye as hollow, desolate, inadequate. A cross not worth bearing.

A deeper absence will open in the human heart.

The teacher watches him leave. What the rich young man did not see that day, what he could not see behind his back, was the face of the Son of Man. Gravity has pulled his face to a frown. Sadness has welled up like beads of sweat on his brow. It will be a long few minutes before he too silently turns to walk again the opposite direction, the empty road.

The next step in the bearing of one's cross—after admitting failure and being made last—is to face rejection, to seek after absence for what the human heart lacks.

He had great wealth.

Many times I've pondered this fact. By American standards, I am certainly not rich. But by global standards, every cent any household makes over $38,000 per year places it among the world's wealthiest 1 percent. And by the standards of first-century Palestine, I am obscenely wealthy. I can't seem to shake the notion that I am likely more wealthy than the rich young man who ran to meet the Son of Man.

So what does this fact make of me?

In the light of his long walk home, nothing I can do seems like rejection enough before the words of the Son of Man. All of it, all of me, is absence.

As I walk away, out of the labyrinth, I see the first flying bat of the season dip and glide from tree to tree. The light is dimming fast. Along the long walk home, two other bats dive low. I duck and shudder. By the time I reach home, the street lights are the only light left to see by. Standing on the sidewalk in front of my home, an unresolved sadness fills the absences of my heart.

He went away sad. The man turns away to walk the long walk home. In all the history of the world, it seems the saddest circle of a path ever walked.

If the disciples would but turn their heads, they would see the rich young man walking away in the distance. He grows smaller and smaller with each step.

But Jesus is pushing ahead.

His disciples leave everything behind to keep pace.

part six

The Things We Keep and Leave Behind

As this story will go, I experienced a profound failure, a devastating rejection, along the path of my vocation, my sense of calling. And it happened in the exact same place where I experienced epiphany amid tragedy on September 11.

Perhaps the failure was inevitable, because this life in which we rehearse our various trusts—trusting in people and places as broken and frail as ourselves—inevitably fails us.

It started with a church controversy. And, unwittingly, the organization I worked for got caught in the middle of it. You probably don't need me to tell you that the worst kind of politics is the politics one often finds in the church, often needlessly destructive, recklessly petty, ridiculously mean-spirited. For reasons that aren't worth explaining here, I spent a whole season of my life doing crisis management for the organization. I sat in innumerable meetings. I helped draft press releases. And I spent most of my time listening to phone calls and responding to e-mails, some from people who were reasonably irate, others from people who were in an irrational rage.

It took its toll. I was not a happy human being.

And then, nearly a year later, just as things seemed to be calming down, the economics of the time caught up with the organization.

And I was laid off.

I was joined by fifteen or so other friends and coworkers. It was a strange day, that day in May. But it wasn't completely unexpected. Everyone knew something was coming. I had turned down the possibility of a lateral move within the organization a few months prior. It came with the hint that my present position was vulnerable. I turned it down because, in my heart of hearts, I knew I needed more of a change than that.

But that knowledge didn't make any of it any easier.

I know I have forgotten many of the details of that day, the time that led up to it and the time after it. Maybe that's a good thing. Maybe the forgetting is just as crucial as the remembering. The things we forget, and the fact that we have forgotten them, are just as important as the things we remember and the fact that we remembered them.

It is a strange thing, a surreal feeling, to be laid off. I don't know if I can describe it. It is a surreal feeling to know that you are being "let go" (surreal, too, the language we use), let go not because you haven't performed well, nor because you aren't valuable to the organization, but because of circumstances and consequences that are far beyond your control. You are being let go "without cause." I remember being told that my position was eliminated only because it was in the executive director's office and the executive director had to lead by example.

I still have the recommendation letter from the executive director, attesting to my skills, talent, experience and performance.

Surreal.

Surreal, the things we remember and forget, the things we keep and leave behind.

I remember packing my cubicle in a rush because I was supposed to be out of the building by noon. I remember that my brother had just returned home from college and he helped me pack. I remember moving so fast that it seemed only like a new project I was working on, as if I were on autopilot. I remember, months later, discovering that I had left behind things in my office that I should have kept.

It wasn't until I got home that afternoon and pressed the play button on the answering machine that the reality of it overwhelmed me. There was one new message.

The one new message was from my pastor. He had mentored me through numerous stages in my life. He had counseled and married my wife and me. He always seemed to be there, in the right place, with the right word, at the right time. And to this day, I have no idea how he was able to find out so fast what had happened. It had happened only a few hours before.

But at the sound of one word from his voice—his compassionate, steadfast, loving-kind voice—I lost it. I cannot remember a word of what he said, but his voice is as clear as light in my mind.

At the sound of his voice, I lost it.

I was standing in our kitchen listening to our answering machine, and I was weeping.

It would be a long number of days, months, feeling the in-betweenness of everything in life. Somehow, I think we think it is more comforting to say we are "in between jobs" than "out of work." And indeed, it didn't take long to start to line up some freelance work to keep occupied, if even a little bit, which only meant I was "in between jobs" more often.

So much of my life I had spent in liminal spaces, at the threshold of wrestling with my vocation, and now I found myself at a threshold made too real, almost unbearable.

I remember in those days and months being haunted by a lyric—another fragment of a line—by the band Coldplay. I remember how it resonated with me, how it seemed to sum up the whole of my life up to that point. Something about how nobody says life will be easy, but nobody tells you it will be this hard either.

All this in-betweenness made itself most manifest in frequent nights of insomnia, my heart burning with trouble, my mind swimming in a sleepless alchemy of stress, anxiety and endless questioning. I have experienced intermittent echoes of sleeplessness ever since, whenever worry or pressure rises to its most acute levels. It is my body's lingering memento of this in-between time in my life.

Yes. I knew it wouldn't be easy. But I didn't know it could be this hard. This surreal life, running in circles.

And yet if facing failure is the first step to bearing a cross, and if facing rejection is the one thing I lack, then maybe this is the last step to the center of the path, to be emptied of all that would stand in the way.

Of course, there was another surreal turn in the story. One of the "benefits" (surreal, the language we use) we received as part of our severance package was a set number of hours of outplacement counseling and training. So a week or two after my last day at work, I received a call from the outplacement firm. The name of the woman on the other end of the line was Tanya Scott. I can remember her name because I still have the folder in the basement of our home, the same folder that still contains five copies of my recommendation letter, surreal mementos.

I remember having several awkward conversations with her about the future of my career, about what services her firm could offer me. Or at least I felt awkward having them. I can honestly remember thinking how my life seemed to be coming straight out of the movie *Office Space*, which at least gave me the comfort of being able to laugh at it.

But then, at one point, she asked me about furthering my education. And when she said she could use the remaining hours allotted to me to research graduate programs and provide me with a file of information to act upon, I was energized by the invitation. I assembled a list of places and programs that would interest me, and a couple of weeks later, a thick manila envelope arrived in the mail. Some of the information I already knew, but now, at this twist in the path of my life, it came to me again, for the first time, almost as if it were completely new.

This was how I came to finally apply to seminary, to respond to the call that I had felt—and that others had felt in me—for years. Less than a year later, my wife and I packed our whole lives into a truck and drove eighteen hours to the new life that awaited us in New Haven, Connecticut, and I enrolled at Yale Divinity School.

Not quite four years after that, on the festival of Epiphany, I was called and ordained a minister of the Word of God.

In hindsight now, as I tell the story, as I write it down, it seems a little too good to be true. It would be all too easy to give this part of the story of my life a shallow moral. It would be all too easy to give it some variation on the cliché that *all things turn out for good.* It would be all too easy, when the fact of the matter is, if I was experiencing any sense of the divine at all during that time, I was experiencing the *Deus absconditus,* the absent God, the hidden God, the forsaken God. And to stick a moral at the end of this part of the story would only heap another broken cliché on a heap of broken ideas of what it means to follow after the God who is lost in absence.

The deepest value, as I see it now, to facing failure and rejection, its struggle and suffering, is to experience the way it strips away the human heart until all that is left is sheer trust. This is hope in its starkest, and most revealing, light.

We too easily forget that in Robert Frost's most famous poem, the road *less traveled by* is actually a cause less for celebration than for regret. We have forgotten that the poem is actually quite lonely, almost despondent. The poet himself ends in a *sigh* infused with doubt, exhausted by the unavoidable choices of his former youth. It sighs with the realization that once we choose one path, others are necessarily forsaken, left behind. And there can be no turning back. For the poet, this is the definition of regret. And as it turns out, the *difference* at the end of the poem just might be the sign that says *dead end.*

And it is exactly at this moment when any "practical atheism" we have left gives way to our true gods—to that which our heart most deeply desires—and the false gods simply evaporate into the ether. And we are left empty, stripped bare. In this absence we are experiencing the *Deus absconditus,* the absent God, the hidden God, the forsaken God.

And the heavy weight digging into our shoulder is the beam of a cross.

This can be a horrifying realization. It can imprison us with its stark-naked reality. It can leave us at the debilitating threshold in between the fear that we will never arrive at what we thought life would be like and the worry that perhaps we arrived at the best point in our life a long time ago.

To stand at this threshold is to stand at the point of paralysis. On the one hand, I can be paralyzed by nostalgia, by the feeling that my best days are days gone by. This isn't a paralysis reserved only for the old. I can remember the year after I graduated from college, going back to campus for homecoming and wondering if those years might have already been the best years of my life. For a moment, I was nearly paralyzed by nostalgia.

On the other hand stands the paralysis of anticipation, the sense that everything will be better in the days, months, years from now. I can feel this paralysis now, in the often exhausting work of parenting, already dreaming ahead to what I think I might feel at my son's graduation, looking to escape the hard work of parenting him through the childhood that will get him from here to there, overlooking the small joys sitting right before me, in the everyday. It is easy to be paralyzed by our anticipation of what might sooner or later be.

In either case, in these times of struggle and suffering, freeing ourselves from the horror that threatens to paralyze us depends on what we see or don't see right before our very eyes. It depends on our willingness to take one step in front of the other, and then to be willing to stand in the center of our emptiness, in the trust that there can still be an unspeakable joy hidden in every present moment, that there can still be peace hidden like glue in the cracks in between the already and the not-yet of our lives.

As I look back to the aftermath of those nine months, and the two years that preceded them, this is how I learned to become attentive. This is how my mind was stripped down to the kind of acuity that recognizes the little details. This was when my eyes, my ears and all my senses were tuned to the tinier chords that the overwhelming world is otherwise oblivious to. Suffering keens the senses. It sharpens all our ways of knowing and perceiving the world down to the tiniest point in the eye of the needle.

And yet I still sometimes wonder why, after all I endured in those nine months and the two years that preceded them, I would still feel called to an even deeper involvement with the dysfunctional family we call the church. I don't have an answer to my own question, at least not one that I can put in the words of a moral at the end of the story. Except to say that the church—even in its deepest failures—can still point us to the hidden God who lives within failure and rejection, who sits at the threshold, to be made manifest in the lives of those who have been rejected and forsaken.

When I finally entered divinity school, I was struck by the number of people who cherished the words of Frederick Buechner as much as I did. I have long cherished the keen perception and wisdom, and the turn of phrase, that I find in Buechner's writing. But people in seminaries and divinity schools are fond of quoting one particular sentence from Buechner about vocation. It has reached the status of a proverb. It can show up in prospective student visits. It can hang on doors of faculty offices. It is a sentence that I too have cherished deeply, even long before I stepped into divinity school. It comes from his book *Wishful Thinking*, and it goes like this: "The place God calls you to is the place where your deep gladness and the world's deep hunger meet."

It carries the poignancy of wisdom, doesn't it? Even now I find myself drawn to it. I get caught up in its lyrical symmetry. It is hard not to get swept up in its simple, near-perfect math.

But that is also its problem, the math of it. How do we determine the world's deep hunger? And how do we know if our gladness is deep enough to meet it? As it often turns out, I am afraid that the math of it, the formula by which anyone may determine their greatest joy, let alone the world's deepest need, is virtually impossible.

And what about those times when meeting the world's hunger requires of me something other than what makes me glad? And what if the gladness can be known only through the hunger?

At any given point in time, we are called to any given number of relationships and actions in the world. We are called to be a child, a sibling or a parent; called to work, to study, to rest, to play; called to be a friend, a neighbor, a colleague, even a stranger. I know I am answering God's call when I begin to see how the various relationships and actions of my life—who I am, what I am doing—coalesce within the power of God's loving-kindness. I am answering God's call when these various relationships and actions begin to mutually bless each other without any effort of my own. It just happens. It happens when being a husband makes me a better writer. It happens when being a parent makes me a better child. It happens when being a stranger makes me a better friend. Vice versa and ad infinitum. It happens when God's callings upon my life move the fragments of me into a deeper wholeness, from solipsism to mutuality, from myself to my neighbor. And the total of them becomes exponentially greater than the sum of their parts.

I have found myself, more and more, drawn to a sense of calling that has no proverb to accompany it, no simple math. It is the day-by-day work of perceiving the little fractures and failures in the lives that stand right before my eyes, and then to enter into their brokenness, not with a moral to end their story but with a courage to take the next step with them, to encounter the life I will find only by walking together with them into it. This calling has no simple math or symmetry, because we know it most often by its messiness, its particular peculiarities, its quotidian details.

Details like the timbre of a voice on an answering machine. Like the name of a woman who, years ago, spent a few hours of her life to research the future of mine. Like the gob of spit made into mud rubbed into a blind eye to make it see again, for the first time.

In short, this calling is a labyrinth all its own, a singular path that contains multitudes. I walk it in the prayer to take one step in front of the other, in the simple discernment of whatever might be the next little act in this life we are given, in all its failures, hunger and gladness.

29

Labor

OVERNIGHT, THE STORM PASSED THROUGH. The air is cool once again. A month ago the storm front would have made things cold, but now the day is cool, pleasantly cool.

Spring has taken hold.

A robin flies from tree to tree where the bat had been the night before. I begin to walk in the cool air. The churchyard has yet to be mowed since the onset of winter. And the rain has made the grass grow differently in different places. In some spots the grass is long. In others it is still stubble.

The rain has brought out a new field of blossoming weeds too. This time their blossoms are white.

There are times I walk the labyrinth and wish there were some way to transcribe the words—thoughts, ideas, images—that pass through my mind. To compose the stream of consciousness as it happens, like ticker tape passing through one ear and out the other, ticking off the streaming words. I feel this way today. But the task is impossible. The technology does not exist.

On a deeper level, the problem is beyond technology.

Because the problem is in the waiting in between the thinking of words and their writing, in the finding and the losing, the keeping and the leaving behind, of words. I must wait to write the words. I must wait until I am in a place where I can truly write them. And the dissonance between the thought word and the written word can be astonishing.

In algebra, the numbers are always constant, but the letters are variable. This is the cognitive dissonance at the center of the problem. This is the algebraic formula of the problem of letters, words and their writing.

And so I will write what I know and what I know I have lost: thoughts, ideas, images. The time in between the walking and the sitting, in between the thinking and the writing, will burn away some of the words. New words will arise from their ashes.

Writing this is labor, hard labor.

It will be simultaneously joy and sorrow, remembering and forgetting, and labor, hard labor, this knowledge without knowledge.

But I can have it no other way.

After an hour of walking and silence, he turns around to face the disciples (Mk 10:23-31 NIV). But he keeps walking. The teacher is walking backwards before them on the way to Jerusalem. He faces his disciples walking behind him.

His disciples await the stream of words from the mouth of their teacher.

How hard it is for the rich.

Jesus is still contemplating the sad young man. *Children, how hard it is.* And then the parable of a camel through the eye of a needle.

The disciples' astonishment is made strange by the surreal, grotesque image of Jesus' words: camels strained through needles, blood and bowels and entrails sloshing the floor, a thin thread of camelhair pulled through the eye's other side.

How hard it is to see the life of God with wealth in your eyes, but how easy it is to fancy the giving up of it. As difficult as the teaching is, I can feel a sheen of comfort in it. As little as I have of wealth, on a certain deep level I yearn to be done with it all. With money come trouble and stress and more toil. The calculating of value. The reckoning of debt.

The checkbook I balanced this morning. The bills I paid. The opening of the envelope of financial statements. The surprise or the angst of the numbers I find there. The numbers are constant, constantly streaming.

All the numbers to balance and check.

All the numbers to pay and withhold.

All the numbers to numb the mind.

The numbers are constant. But the letters are variable. My son is now loving to learn the alphabet, but so far he refuses to learn numbers. I cannot blame him. I would love to be done with the numbering of what I have accumulated and lost.

Nevertheless, can I have it another way? Who can live without the numbers, the giving and the taking, the tallying in black and red, the rules of exchange?

This is the way the world is ordered. It is a zero-sum game.

Thus the question that arises from the back of the circle. It starts as a murmur, becoming a chorus. Its number is constant.

Who then can be saved?

Indeed, this is the crux—the cross—of the matter. After all the hard teaching, first and last, marriage and divorce, riches and renunciation: Who then can be saved?

I am afraid the answer is none. Its number is zero, a zero-sum game.

But in between the question and the answer, in between the numbers and letters, Jesus opens a new window into the reign—the labor—of God.

For mortals impossible, but not for God.

All things are possible with God.

If my answer is zero, then in the utter void of the number that has no number is the promise. Its sign is a circle. The disciples gather around their teacher in this circle. Jesus stands at the center. His value is the labyrinth of value. Its promise is found in the opposite of zero.

If it is impossible for those who are finite, it is possible for the One who is infinite. If it is impossible for those who are not god, it is possible for the One who is.

Who can be saved when I am doing the saving? Zero.

Who can be saved when God is doing the saving? Only God knows.

It is expressed in the reversal of numbers, in the renunciation of the zero-sum calculation that orders the world. This is how the first are made last, the many are made the few.

In the promise, God creates again infinity from the void, presence in absence. The reign of God is the beginning of all things, created and re-created. It is an infinite-sum game. It turns over and over again in the labyrinth of the possibility of God. It expresses itself in the turning of things on its head. The constants are variable. The variables are constant. The first now last. The last now first.

At the center of the square made a circle is the promise within the emptiness of zero.

For God all is possible.

Funny that I remember now, as if I had forgotten, that in the ancient etymology of words, *labor* and *labyrinth* share the same roots. Ancient writers writing of the labyrinth—Ovid and Virgil among them—will make a pun of the words. Their double meanings will abound.

The labyrinth is a tortuous labor to walk. Labor is an unending labyrinth of work.

And the word *labor* will share the labyrinth's double meaning. As the labyrinth signifies simultaneously the skilled artistry of its construction and the chaotic confusion of its path, so labor signifies both the continually grueling process of work and the finally crafted product the work produces.

In it all, there is both pain and pleasure, joy and sorrow, remembering and forgetting.

And yet there is another meaning still. In labor, hard labor, is the giving birth to something new, new life born of the womb. Labor and labyrinth madc onc in childbirth.

As I walk to the center, I hear the sound of children through the open window of the church building, its only open window. This is a day for open windows, a sign of spring. The sound of the children is the babbling sound of playing. They play an infinite-sum game, the infinite promise hidden within a zero.

The babbling is the sound of thoughts, ideas, images, overflowing my mind.

I walk the labyrinth, a labor waiting for words and their writing.

Somewhere, I imagine, my child is learning the alphabet, all its letters.

30

The Path

I LEAVE FOR THE LABYRINTH NEAR DUSK. The smell of barbecue is heavy in the air. I have eaten already, but a twinge of hunger tickles my stomach. In the steep valleys between houses the western sun trickles through. It reclines eight inches above the earth, slowly descending. I reach the churchyard in the cooling light of evening.

There are churches in northern France that historically named their paved labyrinths the *Chemin de Jérusalem.* The Path to Jerusalem. To walk the labyrinth was to walk the way to the holy city standing at the center.

Chemin de Jérusalem. The history behind the name is ambiguous, unknown. But it makes of the labyrinth's geography a metaphorical pilgrimage, a physical metaphor for the longer pilgrimage of the spirit. There is a church in Lille, France, that centuries ago designed a labyrinth for its floor. The plan called for the symbols of cities to be drawn along the pilgrim way. Lille at the entrance. Rome. Constantinople. Jerusalem at the center.

But it stands only as a map, a metaphor. It was never built. Or if it was, it remains undiscovered, known but unknown.

All we have left is the drawing of a design on paper, the metaphor of a pilgrimage.

Jesus' stride is gaining speed (Mk 10:32-34).

The road from the east, moving west to Jerusalem, is uphill. But the long, slow rise does not slow him. A paradox, it hastens his steps. The disciples follow as close as they can. But they are amazed at his quickening pace. Behind them are the crowds, some of whom cannot keep up. They trail into the distance. The fear in them is gaining speed too, and it is palpable. Jesus appears to them now as a phantom riding the wind.

They were amazed, and those who followed were afraid. Jesus can feel the mix of awe and fear bristling the goose bumps up his spine, along his scalp. And perhaps this is the nature of amazement. It is the maze of emotions made of fear mixed with awe.

But will not stop. His breath and his steps are accelerating into a rhythm. The city of cities, the holy city, is close now, high on the horizon. He does not want to stop so close to the end.

So quickly he pulls the Twelve off to the side of the road. He speaks close to them. In the swiftness of the gesture they can feel the weight of the moment, the holy gravity of it pulling them along. Whether they are still walking or standing still, they cannot tell. They are a swirling maze of emotions turning round the Son of Man.

He stretches out his arm and points to the gleaming city. Underneath their conscious thoughts, they knew this is where they are heading. Underneath the fear and awe, they know this will be the end of the road. But Jesus has never uttered its name. All they have followed are his silent steps.

See, we are going up to Jerusalem.

The *Chemin de Jérusalem.*

The unknown is now made known. And it feels as if the prophet is lifting the Twelve up to the sky and flying them to the holy city: the crowded streets, the bustling marketplace, the imposing temple. They see themselves jostling the city. He is opening up to them a vision in the clear mystic air. The details are clear.

The implicit is now made explicit. And the explicit is made more explicit again. For the third time, he repeats the prediction of the Son of Man, his tragic fate. And this third time he fills the foreshadowing with the clear details of action. *Handed over. Condemn. Hand over.*

Mock. Spit upon. Flog. Kill. And then the three days to rise.

The vision has dimmed to bloody darkness, but the details are clear.

He speaks as if the script had already been written. His disciples' attention is keened to the horrifying details. Awe now mixes thoroughly with dread fear. As he resumes his swift step, they are paralyzed by fear.

Supposedly, this was how the *Chemin de Jérusalem* was walked: the pilgrims would approach the labyrinth and fall to their knees. The pilgrims would then waddle the path on their knees. All the while, the pilgrims would sing in prayer.

Tonight, I walk the *Chemin de Jérusalem.* At the entrance to the labyrinth, I crouch to my knees. I waddle the path on my knees, my hips swiveling me forward, my feet swinging from side to side behind me. All the while, I sing the prayers I know by heart, songs for this season.

I sing a song I know full well.

What wondrous love is this, O my soul, O my soul!
What wondrous love is this, O my soul!
What wondrous love is this
That caused the Lord of bliss
To bear the dreadful curse for my soul, for my soul,
To bear the dreadful curse for my soul.

Kneeling in the clear mystic air, I waddle past all the cities that mark the geography of my life, its memory. Maryland Heights, where I spent my littlest years. Manchester, where I became a teenager. Valparaiso, where I went to college. Webster Groves, where I started adulthood and found marriage. New Haven, where we continued our education. The Bronx, where I first preached. University City, where we have now started a family. The cities mark the labyrinth of my life, its vision.

When I was sinking down, sinking down, sinking down,
When I was sinking down, sinking down,
When I was sinking down

Beneath God's righteous frown,
Christ laid aside his crown for my soul, for my soul,
Christ laid aside his crown for my soul.

Along the way, I feel the ground soft beneath me. My knees begin to ache. The muscles in my hips tighten, seize and grow sore. I can feel the ground's moisture seep through to the skin of my knees. There is a thin sheen of mud on my pant legs.

I reach the center.

Jerusalem.

My mind is clear, emptied of useless knowledge. My body relaxes, a holy exhaustion. My whole life is laid before me in the circuits of the path. I kneel in its center.

I remain on my knees to sing the prayer.

To God and to the Lamb, I will sing, I will sing;
To God and to the Lamb, I will sing.
To God and to the Lamb
Who is the great "I Am";
While millions join the theme, I will sing, I will sing;
While millions join the theme, I will sing.

Along the center's edge, on the ground before me, sits a twig. On its end, the twig forks to make a Y. I pick it up as I sing. It is edged with thorns. The tiny thorns are pliable, not nearly severe enough to prick blood. It stands as a metaphor for the end that is yet to come. *Mock. Spit upon. Flog. Kill.* I plant it in the ground as I stand to leave, its arms outstretched, uplifted to the sky.

And when from death I'm free, I'll sing on, I'll sing on;
And when from death I'm free, I'll sing on.
And when from death I'm free,
I'll sing and joyful be;
And through eternity, I'll sing on, I'll sing on;
And through eternity, I'll sing on.

I stand. Back on my feet, I walk the way out of the labyrinth to walk my way home. The lingering light marks my return from Jerusalem to this, my present home, my present life, to the relationships and actions that await me here.

In my mind, the unknown is known. The details are clear.

Along the edge of the churchyard, beside a stone wall, red tulips are in bloom. Beads of scarlet red splash open, pleading to the skies.

31

Running Late

I ARRIVE AT THE LABYRINTH IN HASTE—late—after a late day at work. I have little precious time before evening commitments. Somewhere along the way, I will stop—briefly—to eat. Another day in the life of the frenetic orders of the world. In the car, the radio brings news that Congress and the president have reached a tentative agreement about their budget, about who gets to keep the money they think is theirs. But I am sure they will find something else to fight over tomorrow.

All these zero-sum games.

How to begin in the ways of the world, where every game is competitive, every relation is contested, every word is combative?

I begin by taking the first step in the path. These steps, these first breaths, taken in open air. The gilded light is late in the day. But it radiates the air and the ground with radiant things. I take a second step, and a third, and a fourth.

The labyrinth refuses to be raced. Here, there are no first and last. There is no finish line. All walk the same path. All reach the same center. The labyrinth refuses to become a contest or a competition. It requires only a kind of slow mindfulness. It imparts a quiet attention. It slows time to an order beyond time.

I can feel time slow to a rhythm with half-lit radiance. I can feel existence merge into step with being. The steps merge me with words I've read in my past, words about fly-fishing, about water and the words beneath the babble of water, and about a love beyond understanding.

The timelessness in time flies quickly. As I exit the labyrinth, I stop, turn and bow my head. I submit my day—what it has been and what it is yet to be—to a newfound authority.

For once, they stop—briefly—to eat (Mk 10:35-45 NIV). Stale bread and dried fish. A woman brings them fresh goat's milk, and it is sweet to the taste. They know Jesus will not tarry long. He has already finished his meal and he waits—arms folded, eyes down, thoughts deep—for his disciples. They will walk a mile more before laying their heads on stones to sleep along the road.

They will not dream as they sleep.

The sons of Zebedee have finished eating too. The determination that tightens their faces causes them to rise. They glance at each other and nod. They take Jesus by his arm and corner him along the side of the road.

Do for us whatever we ask. The demand drips with reckless ambition. And with irony. They do not know what they ask. And they do not know that they do not know.

Can you drink the cup I drink? Jesus asks the question with enough bite that the others overhear it. James and John wince. Their scheme is exposed, into the light, into open air.

The question turns into a pronouncement. *You will drink the cup I drink.* Jesus says the words with such dread conviction, with such sober forewarning, that the brothers' ambition instantly distills to regret. Now they know what they did not know.

As for the other ten, their own ambition ferments to jealous indignation.

Quickly, Jesus finds himself in the middle, the referee of an escalating brawl. James and John have their backs to each other, their fists raised to fight. The mosh pit of disciples is shoving and pushing.

Then comes the voice, loud:

You know.

The deep boom of his voice freezes them all.

You know that those who are regarded as rulers of the Gentiles lord it over them.

His arms are extended. One hand points to one horizon, to Herod's palace beside Jerusalem. The other points to Rome, unseen beyond the other horizon.

His voice breaks them back into reality. They stand under the thumb of the empires of the world, already last. They are fighting a fight someone else already won.

The true powers of the world laugh at their petty fighting.

All the frenetic orders of the world. All these zero-sum games.

They remember again: the whole reason they follow this man is the way he has resurrected their dignity, the way he undoes this oppression with one sound of his voice.

He speaks again, now with gentle conviction, his extended arms encircling them.

Not so with you.

Among them—among them all—the great are the servants, and the greatest are the slaves of all. Life turned again on its head. True life found in its paradox. Real life found among its last and its least.

And then Jesus speaks the truth that makes sense of it all.

For even the Son of Man did not come to be served, but to serve.

He hesitates in the weight of the moment.

And to give his life as a ransom for many.

Now everything is fully known.

He will die not simply to die the death required by tragedy, by its drama. He dies to turn tragedy's fate on its head. He dies the death of one for the life of many.

The slow sense it makes of the moment is fleeting, as the silence of the moment passes. Timelessness flies in time. Jesus breaks his stance to run in the late half-light again, one more mile before he lays his head to rest. They quicken to follow.

As he runs ahead of them, his face to the wind, no soul can see his eyes, bloodshot with sadness.

32

But Now I See

I LEAVE FOR THE LABYRINTH AFTER THE SUN HAS SET. The sky is deepening to indigo. The electric light I walk by draws circles of streetlight against asphalt. The moon stands in high relief in the sky, gleaming with reflected light, glowing with a halo of misty white light.

The air darkens with each step.

I reach the churchyard.

I stop at its border.

Two bats are swooping and swooning through the labyrinth. I wait and I watch. They spiral and swirl in wheeling circuits, up high, then down low. For a few minutes, I keep waiting and I keep watch.

But I am spooked. I cannot make myself climb up the hill to the labyrinth.

Tonight they fly the labyrinth. I leave them to their flying path.

I turn to leave the labyrinth behind. I feel dejected to leave it behind.

No. I feel like I am the one left behind.

Then the thought emerges almost like a memory. I walk this walk not to twist and turn on a path made of brick.

I walk this path to see the labyrinth in every path.

So tonight the labyrinth I walk is the walk to the churchyard and the walk back home, the turns along walkways, the twists through streets. The neighborhood is a labyrinth. The city is a labyrinth. The world is a labyrinth. All the paths spiral the globe in fateful circuits.

Tonight I stand at the edge of the outskirts of Jerusalem, the city of cities, the holy city. I walk along the edge of mystery, steeped in darkness. I am walking back to the center, my home.

All my ways lead there.

All along the way to Jerusalem, they pass time by taking turns telling stories (Mk 10:46-52 NIV). They are reminiscing. For whatever awaits them in Jerusalem, they will have these memories to live by. They spend half the night in Jericho telling stories. Their rabbi sits with them and listens, staring at the ground and smiling. Jericho, on the outskirts of the holy city. Jericho, with its seven circuits of walls, a labyrinth of a city. Jericho, the ancient story of a chosen people walking the walls down in tortuous circuits.

They are sitting on the edge of the city, in darkness, on the edge of the mystery it will contain. They are telling stories together. They know them so well they can finish each other's sentences.

Like the time it all began. Remember? Bethsaida, wasn't it? Yes, Bethsaida. The blind beggar. Remember how the crowds dragged him along like a rag doll? (A few of them snicker.) Remember how the rabbi spat on the ground? (A disciple clears his throat and spits in parody. They laugh.) Remember what the rabbi said? (Jesus smiles every time they mention him as if he weren't there.) *Do you see anything?* Remember the old beggar's reply? *I see people. They look like trees walking around* (Mk 8:23-24 NIV).

The circle of disciples explodes in laughter. Even Jesus laughs, his shoulders shaking with stifled laughter. For whole minutes of time, they laugh together. Just when it seems to die down, it erupts again.

Until one of them asks. Whatever happened to that old beggar?

What was his name?

In the lonely dance of candlelight, the room quiets. They stare at the rabbi staring at the ground. Not one of the disciples knows or remembers his name.

On my way back home, I take the long way. I reminisce, telling myself the stories memory makes of the past. All the days before this one. The first day, the first step. The praying. The tending of grounds. The changing of seasons. The walking on knees.

I remember the time, nearly two years ago, when a bat swooped into our home. We nearly died with fright. But our child slept through the night. Only now can I laugh at the story memory has made of it.

On the way back home, I sing my prayer.

Amazing grace! How sweet the sound
That saved a wretch like me.
I once was lost, but now am found,
Was blind, but now I see.

Through many dangers, toils, and snares
I have already come.
'Tis grace hath brought me safe thus far,
And grace will lead me home.

All my ways lead from here to there, the home made of grace.

They leave Jericho early. It will be a steep climb to Jerusalem. The city gleams before them in high relief, glowing with a misty halo of morning light. A crowd now joins the pilgrim journey.

Then the voice, high and piercing. *Jesus, Son of David, have mercy on me!* The disciples are stunned. The secret is out, even here on the edge of the city of cities. Powerful people can hear it. The crowd rushes to hush the voice, but it will not be stilled.

Son of David, have mercy!

Jesus bids the little one to stand. The blind beggar throws off his coat. The blind beggar springs up. The blind beggar now stands before Messiah.

The last now stands before the first.

What do you want me to do for you? John and James look at each other and wonder.

Rabbi, I want to see. The blind beggar speaks with the matter of facts.

Go. Your faith has healed you.

No spit. No walking trees. The man simply opens his eyes. With a shining clarity, he sees the face of the Son of David.

The first now stands before the last.

It has been so long since the disciples have witnessed his power that they had forgotten the wonder of it all. A blind man sees.

Yes. A blind man sees.

This time will be the last time. They stand at the edge of Jerusalem. There the mystery of the secret will be revealed for all to see.

And this time the blind beggar will not be left behind. The faith made in him has made him to follow.

And all his ways led from here to there, from there to here.

One of the disciples asks him his name.

His name is Bartimaeus.

33

Heartbeat

I WALK THE LABYRINTH EARLY, BEFORE WORK. I walk while there is a respite in the rain. The forecast calls for rain all day, and with it a chill. There are hints of both in the draft of air in the churchyard.

The water brings new color to the life living on land. Clear water contains within it the full spectrum of color. The dogwoods are in full bloom, broken open in white. Tiny cross-shaped labyrinths in bloom. The grass is livening to its most vibrant green.

Life is growing.

Clover, moss, grass—all green with life—begin to overgrow the circles of brick.

But the path is still clear enough to walk. I walk the wet ground. I spot a cardinal—red with brown and a beak of orange—gliding through the churchyard. The bird perches in the dogwood tree, red amid white.

Life—the full spectrum of its color—is growing.

The hike up to the city's limits was rigorous (Mk 11:1-11). But now they stand outside the gate. What seemed so imposing in the distance now squats before them, life-size, concrete, real. The crowd around them is growing large, fellow pilgrims approaching for Passover. Galileans are greeting neighbor Galileans, familiarity found in far-off places.

But Jesus has stayed ahead of the crowd, if just a few steps ahead. He stands before the gate, his back to the crowd. Two disciples hold the colt by a tether before him. The colt stomps. The rest of the disciples and the crowd gape at him. They see the rabbi's shoulders and torso heave wide with air. They see him inhale the wind, whole and entire. He holds the breath for a moment. Then the exhale, and everything drops. Shoulders, arms, ribs, spine. They see the muscles under his tunic relax. He stands now at the threshold. When he crosses over, it is the end of the road.

The Son of Man has reached the end of the open road.

Everything, everything that had moved so swiftly, so *immediately*, to this one point now slows, now stops. Time slows and stops. They have climbed the ascent to the center of earth, the city of cities, and everything slows to the beat of his heart. In the slowing silence, they can hear the slowing beat of his heart.

Ba-thump. Ba-thump. Ba-thump.

Ba-thump. Ba-thump.

Ba-thump.

And then with one swift swoop, he is astride the colt. And for this once, for this one time, he is off his feet.

For this one and only time, he moves without walking. This is the first sign of the Son of Man at the gates of Jerusalem.

And the second sign is more miraculous than the first. The unridden colt accepts the rider, willingly. The rabbi pats the colt on the side of his neck and, with the sound of a sweet kiss in the air, bids him to walk. The step is assured and unwild. Those standing closest to the colt could swear he is stepping to the beat of the heart of the Son of Man.

And then, from the middle of the crowd comes the shout of one voice.

Hosanna! And *Hosanna* again.

The word booms like thunder in the air. The disciples know the voice. The crowd knows the voice.

The voice belongs to Bartimaeus.

Bartimaeus shouts the saving cry of the Son of David, the Son of Man.

The crowd soon follows, and shouts surge through the body electric.

And imitating the one who called him David's son, in homage to the

One who is David's son, they throw off their cloaks.

Bartimaeus laughs. Jesus smiles. The cloaks of those who once blind now see strew the way of Messiah. The colt strides the patchwork carpet of a carpenter king.

Blessed is the one who comes in the name of the Lord! The people begin singing the psalm outside the gates of the city. The people are dancing in circles around the colt and his rider. The people swing a whirling dervish around the Son of David. Songs of freedom—jubilant freedom—burst forth at the sight of the man.

This morning sings with light at the sight of the captive free.

The gates to the city swing open. The pilgrims—from Galilee and other backwaters—stream in. Jesus and his labyrinthine dervish cross the threshold. Jesus rides in its whirling center.

But soon, too soon, the momentum of song will be dispersed by the crowded cacophony of life in the city.

This morning sings with light.

Jesus walks the labyrinth of the city—the *Chemin de Jérusalem*—the turns through streets and side streets, walkways and alleys, to the center of the city. All this long journey, he has been walking the labyrinth. Back and forth, twist and turn, ebb and flow. All the cities along the way: Galilee and Caesarea and Judea. Jesus walks the labyrinth. He rides it in mystery. He is its prophet, its rabbi, its Christ.

I walk it with him, a whirling dervish.

I walk the labyrinth with the Son of David.

He now stands in the center. He stands in Jerusalem. The long-awaited arrives in the long-awaiting city. He brings in his wake the reign of God, from the margins to the center.

I stand now in the center of the labyrinth with the Son of Man.

Little did I know it, but he has walked with me every day, all along the way.

He now stands in the center of the center. He looks around. He takes in everything whole. The temple shimmers in the setting sun, its rooms and halls and courtyards a tortuous maze. Whispers of hosanna echo faintly in the distance, then die. The day is coming to a close. The marketers are closing up shop. A man mutters something about fame and money.

Jesus heaves a second great sigh. His muscles tighten. His face flushes. Blood rushes his veins, hot and angry.

I look around in the dissipating half-light before rain. I take in things, partial and incomplete. The church stands tall before me. Winslow's Home crouches behind me, not yet open for the day's business. Cars zoom along a busying street.

I stand at the center of the center with the Son of Man, his burnt face flushed a cardinal red against walls of white stone.

My breath is shallow. All I can hear is the beat of a heart, a tortuous rhythm.

34

Near and Not Far

COLD HAS RETURNED, the ides of March near the end of April. Tomorrow is Palm Sunday. Holy Week will begin. The late season cannot escape its more familiar chill.

I wait until the afternoon, hoping for sun and for warmth.

They do not come. So I walk in the cold. The wind is harsh, a slap in the face. The day has withdrawn back into hibernation. No birds. No squirrels. No walking life.

Only one neighbor is vainly trying to mow his lawn. I hear the whir of the machine but do not see him. The tulip blooms along the wall are nearly all gone. The lone remaining petals curl and shiver.

The walk to the labyrinth is short—not far—and yet has never felt farther.

Cold, I enter the cold labyrinth. Tiny beads of water shiver on the clover. The churchyard, like the day, is vacant. Even the cars on the street shiver in slower time. I want to walk faster than I am, to warm my body. But the cold is thick and slows me down.

At the center, I stand and pray.

I shiver and I pray.

My mind is as vacant as the ground, as vacant as air. Across the street, a blue flag whips in the wind. The tops of the trees writhe in wind. I feel the slap against my face once again.

I walk my way out. My muscles have loosened. My pace picks up. My nose starts to run. I snort the phlegm and spit. It flies and lands beyond the circle.

I pick up a stick as I exit the path.

For the first time, I look and see: the heap of sticks I gathered weeks gone by, left at the feet of the wooden man, is gone. Someone has been here. I cannot say when.

After Jesus entered the city in triumph, after he cleared the temple in disgust, today is the day given over to teaching, to parables, to debate (Mk 12:28-37).

The day is long and drawn out, questions and answers, and more questions still. These are not the backwater rabbis of Galilee. These are the urbane scholars of the city. The lawyers ask about authority. The Pharisees probe his politics. The Sadducees question theology.

Ironies abound. But the carpenter-turned-rabbi is up to the test.

A teacher of the law stands at the edge of the circle. He has hardly moved the whole day long. He leans against the threshold. He listens. He takes note of the answers he hears. Occasionally, he looks down to the ground and smirks at the answers. He knows they are good.

And only now he asks the question: *Which commandment is the first of all?*

Jesus smirks. He had already taken note of the teacher standing at the edge. He is not surprised that he asks the question of questions, the question at the center of them all.

The question is good. It is worth a good answer.

The answer is as old as the ages of ages.

Hear, O Israel. The Lord our God, the Lord is one.

The answer is as old as their childhood, as old as their people. The Shema. The answer of answers. The prayer of prayers. He prayed the prayer upon the rising up of morning. He will pray it again lying down at night.

He knows too that from the Shema flows the greatest commandment, the command of commands. *Love the Lord your God with all your heart, and with all your soul, and with all your mind, and with all your strength. . . . Love your neighbor as yourself.*

The rabbi has summed up the whole law in a prayer and a command.

His answer is good.

The temple still towers over them. The incense of burnt flesh fills the air. The bleat of a goat echoes in the hall. The answer is good, greater still than the sacrifice.

You are not far from the kingdom of God. The teacher tilts his head at the words of the rabbi. Their curiosity furrows his brow. They are filled with the burning incense of mystery.

The asking of questions is now done. No one will dare ask him an open question again.

Does he know? Do the scholars all know?

This is the answer of answers.

The reign of God stands before them in a man, near and not far.

Near and not far, this labyrinth has stood before me. All season long, it has stood.

This much I know about it, about its particularity, its history. It was built in 1997, in celebration of the congregation's 180th anniversary. In the span of time and history, this path is an infant. And yet it is the oldest labyrinth in the city, part of a newfound revival.

And yet its pattern is older still. The congregation's spiritual director at the time designed it from a mosaic found in the basilica of San Vitale in Ravenna, Italy, a labyrinth rumored to be as old as the sixth century or as late as the sixteenth. Its reenactment in this churchyard was to be the first step in a larger memorial garden. But now, fourteen years later, only the path stands.

Laid in black-and-white marble, the original Ravenna labyrinth is modest in size, about eleven feet in diameter. It is a study in geometry: a circle within a much larger octagon, its path marked by circuits of triangles. The triangles seem to give the path direction and movement, arrow points leading out from the center. It is a pattern of patterns. Its pattern now stands before me, circles of brick thatched in crisscrossed blades of grass.

By its pattern, this path—nearer to me, not far—transcends space. I walk this day the centuries-old path of San Vitale in Ravenna.

By its pattern, this path—nearer to me, not far—transcends time. I walk this day the path of Ravenna pilgrims centuries old, long gone. Their cold breath meets mine in cold air.

All things are brought together here in the pattern of questions and answers, the question of questions and the answer of answers. All things are brought here, in this particular place, this particular time, this churchyard, this cold day.

I stand here, a stick in my hand, at the center of all things. I shiver in the familiar presence of unknown things made known, this past held in the hand of this future.

Eternity is here in its particulars, near and not far.

part seven

The Way of the Cross

So where will this path leave me now, the path of my life, the path of these forty days?

You know by now, near the end, that I walk this labyrinth not because I am presently undergoing some great ordeal, nor because I yearned for some great revelation to charge new meaning in my life. This journey started in simple curiosity. Walking this labyrinth was an everyday decision to enter into an everyday routine, a discipline for the everyday. I entered into it seeking something, because in a sense we are always seeking. Too many questions are never completely answered. And too many answers lead only to more questions. The more we ask them, the more we may find the meaning in simply asking the question. The answers become an invitation to enter more deeply into the mystery at the center.

And yet walking this labyrinth brings me more deeply into the whole of my life, the whole of life itself. Just as its circuits push forward to turn back, and turn back to push forward, the labyrinth has pushed me back into my past to turn me forward into the future. From the past into the future. To the future through the past. So many memories have flickered in my mind as I have walked this path. I have recounted some of them here. Some of them remain hidden there, untold. This is how the labyrinth, the labyrinth in life, lives in the present, always a turning between future and past.

Søren Kierkegaard supposedly once wrote, "Life can only be understood backwards, but it must be lived forward." Indeed, only the past is known well enough as to be understood, which does not necessarily mean we understand it. And yet perhaps we can live forward only if we are in some way facing the past, facing up to the point it has brought us in our life.

We can spend so much of our life haunted and consumed by the past, by the way our childhood unfolded, by the demon of a bad decision long gone. Memory can be a mystery, the way it turns us one way, then turns us around again, a labyrinth without a center. Often our life seems to be not our own, only the sum total of what it has been up to this point. And freedom, true freedom, seems as elusive as the wind.

So what do we do with these memories, good and bad, this story memory makes of our lives?

We can psychologize about it. We can write it into the diaries that sit on the nightstands of our life. We can blame it for our problems. We can cherish it for its legacies. We can digitize it into the networks that so fragilely connect us to the other stories memory is making of other lives.

Or we can offer it up to God in prayer, letting it rise before God like incense. In the stillness and silence of prayer, God makes our lives holy, our stories sacred. In prayer, our story becomes God's story. In prayer, God's story becomes our story. This is how God's name is hallowed in our lives. This is how God's kingdom comes into our heart and into our world. This is how God's will in heaven is done on earth. This is how we are given daily bread. This is how we are forgiven. This is how we can forgive. This is how we are led from temptation, and how we are delivered from evil.

Or as Anthony Hopkins confesses, channeling C. S. Lewis in the movie *Shadowlands*: "I pray because I can't help myself. I pray because I'm helpless. I pray because the need flows out of me all the time, waking and sleeping. . . . It doesn't change God. It changes me."

The labyrinth is an empty path. We fill its emptiness, like wine in a wineskin, with every step of ourselves. Every step of ourselves: memories, experience, accomplishments, failures, joys, guilts, tears, laughter, dreams, friendship, hatred, love. Every step of ourselves: the sum total of who we are, where we have been and how we got here. And of that total, some of it is known, some of it unknown, some of it both known and unknown. The total is the mystery of me.

As I face the mystery of the past, the labyrinth pushes me forward into the future.

The labyrinth is a mirror. To stand before it is to stand before the entirety of me. It is impossible for me to tell you all of what streams through my mind, the river of a self's knowledge, even now as I have already told you so much of me. "The world is too much with us," the poet Wordsworth once famously wrote.

In reality, I am too much with me.

Yes, I am too much with me. Here is the irony of our technology, as true for us as it was for Daedalus. The more we are inundated by information—about the world, about ourselves—the less we know about who we truly are, the mystery of us. Information is not yet knowledge, and knowledge is not yet wisdom. But the technologies that proliferate information, even the technologies that make it more *social*, mask this irony, and we are left in a swirling deep of what we think we know about ourselves.

Yes. I am too much with me. We are too much with us.

Of course when we lift the story of our life up to God, we also relinquish our control over it. This may be the hardest part of all. And yet when we relinquish our control over it, we are simultaneously released from its control over us. This is perhaps the most liberating freedom that can be given us, to be released from the double-bind of our past and its control over our present. This is the path to a full and lasting freedom. We walk it with every step of ourselves. We walk it into the ever-abundant presence of God, into the total always greater than the sum of parts.

In this sense, the labyrinth's emptiness is perhaps its greatest power, the way it strips away the knowledge of ourselves, stripping away the accretions of our lives. It does this, first, by facing us up to the irony of our own self-image. It is impossible for me to tell you the sum total of me, or for you to tell me the sum total of you. Words could not bear that weight. It would be too much of us for either of us to know or understand.

And so we tell our stories in glimpses and fragments, as best we can.

Our memories are ultimately only fragments, broken by our forgetting, pieces of a past we are not always even sure is our own. And they remain fragments—a broken story—until they are made whole by prayer. In prayer, God mends the fragments into the art of a life, like stained glass, like a quilt, like cobblestone bricks on a circling path. In prayer, God takes the tortuous turns of my life and turns it once more into a pilgrim's journey, a sublime labyrinth of a life made holy by grace. The empty center of the path of memory is always and can only be grace, a total always greater than the sum of its parts.

In the end, the labyrinth represents this whole journey, this spiraling movement between past and future. This is how the labyrinth becomes a symbol for life, the spiraling present moment, the unending now. Life works in these cycles between doubt and confidence, wandering and direction, failure and freedom, fear and love.

And so really only one question remains: How will this story end? What will push life forward again, breaking the turning and talking in circles, all this back and forth? What will push life forward into new life?

Or is it all simply a ceaseless and exhausting cycle between one and the other?

In a sense, there is only one way this story can end. Perhaps in your heart of hearts you already know how this story will end. There is only one place in the path where past and future can meet in a way that will push life forward anew.

The cross.

The path of the labyrinth is the way of the cross. The cross is the center that is no center at all. Or at least it is the center we would never desire to become the center of life. In the labyrinth, if we are ever to find a divine artistry interwoven in the cosmos, then we must confront the world's most baffling and chaotic disorder. We must confront what remains to be told in the Gospel According to Mark. We must confront the suffering of the world's best-lived, most purpose-driven life, the suffering unto death of the One whose humanity was greater than the sum total of all humankind. We must confront his death as a common criminal, in complete humiliation. This is what makes any and every tragedy—whether on the stage or in life—tragic.

We must come face to face with the cross.

Which means we must confront—face to face—the baffling and chaotic disorders of our own lives. The cross is where my story and Mark's story meet. If the path of the labyrinth is Christ, then Christ is leading me to the cross. The cross is what makes a circle of the square of my life, a sacred geometry.

At the center of the cross is the encounter with the Christ who hangs on it. We follow him all our life, breathlessly chasing after him, and this is the only place where we can nail him down long enough to catch our breath. And here is where he shows us the secret at the center of it all. He shows us the death in life, the life in death, the first in the last, the last in the first.

At the foot of the cross, every paradox comes full circle.

The cross is where death and life meet. We don't know if we will ever really understand it, but the secret of it is here stripped bare for all to see. It is not easy to see.

Thus, we keep looking for the answer to the question.

Buried like a seed in the center of Dietrich Bonhoeffer's classic book *The Cost of Discipleship* lies a sentence so stark in its clarity as to sharpen all things in its focus:

> When Christ calls a man, he bids him come and die.

Here stands the last step in the labyrinth. However many steps we discern in the path to bearing our cross, this is the final step, this death. This is the call that bids us all, women and men. It is the way of the cross.

And it is an invitation that leads to death, the death of the self. The final step in the bearing of my cross is always to die to self. It is the death of the old self in the life and death of the Christ. To become his disciple is to enter into his dying.

But there is a difference in taking this road. There is a difference in this death. This death is not a dead end. This death is a beginning.

Unless a grain of wheat falls into the earth and dies, it remains just a single grain, Jesus says in another Gospel, the Gospel of John (12:24). *But if it dies, it bears much fruit.*

In this death is the rebirth. This kind of death isn't laid in a tomb. It is buried—like a grain of wheat—into the womb of life, into the place where it can be reborn into new life. The labyrinth is its sign, the labyrinth at the threshold of the grave, the labyrinth that draws the anatomy of the womb, the labyrinth of a chrysalis that breaks open to take wing with the wind.

These days, walking this labyrinth, I have begun to feel this life that is reborn in death. I have felt it in its most visceral clarity. I have felt it because my wife and I are expecting. As I have walked this labyrinth, my wife bears in the labyrinth of her womb new life, our second child. It grows within her. We can see with our own eyes the life growing within her. I have kept the fact of this life hidden until now, buried like a seed, like a grain of wheat, but now its life grows near.

Along the way to a cross, we are expecting this new life to be born.

And in just a few months, this new life will be here, face to face.

This is the last, the final, the ultimate and the most radical paradox: that this death is life. A seed buried in the earth. This death is a life given, a ransom for many. Yet, for this death to be the seed that bears fruit in my life, I must die it daily. A daily death to the old self, every day to die. Death to my sin. Death to my brokenness. Death to my pain. Death to my failures. Death too to my successes. Death to all my petty attachments to these zero-sum games the world plays.

A daily death. This is the everyday discipline. This is the answer to the question, and the question at the end of every answer.

This was the death the rich young man could not bring himself to die.

This was the death that opened blind Bartimaeus's sight to see.

This is the death—every day to die—that will push life backwards, then forward to new life again, the chrysalis that breaks open to take wing with the wind.

35

Around and Around

ALL THIS BACK AND FORTH ONCE MORE: the cool warmth of April has returned. The day is golden and half-clear under a smatter of clouds. I walk in the early evening, after work.

Yesterday was Palm Sunday, the Sunday of the Passion. This morning I sat in a chapel and listened to the chanting of the Passion. The plainsong tones were haunting and sublime.

But before I walk to the labyrinth, I have work at home to do. This morning I found a dead squirrel behind a smoke tree in the back of our house. As I look at him now, the squirrel is being flattened by death, the gray-brown hair of his tail matted and limp. But there is no smell, not yet, so the death cannot have been long since. I try to pick it up with a shovel, but the sight of it is too much for me. I lay a newspaper over the carcass.

The squirrel is shrouded by today's news. Death once again is the headline.

I called the animal-control office from work, so I now follow the procedure they laid out for me. I pick up the corpse with a shovel. I put the shrouded body in a trash bag. The body is heavier than I expected for a squirrel. I put the trash bag in another trash bag. I lay the body bag in the trash can.

I go inside to wash my hands of death. Then I leave to walk, to return to life.

With delight. This is how the Jerusalem crowd listens to the rabbi (Mk 12:37-44). He is gaining a following here too. But these are people of the city, urbane and sophisticated. They are not *amazed* or *astonished* with the ecstasies of the illiterate. Rather, refined with culture, they are delighted by the way he turns a phrase, by the way he turns things on their head. He enthralled Galilee with miracles of action. He beguiles Jerusalem with a miracle of words.

Herein lies the conflict. *Beware of the scribes, who like to walk around in long robes.* It is a conflict of authority. The scribes come to authority by the credential of their office. Jesus comes to authority by his own personhood, its charisma.

And Jesus knows the difference between the two. So he saves his most damning words for them. *They devour widows' houses.* Widows: the ones most vulnerable, the ones Torah has pledged them to protect. They are eating the poorest out of house and home.

By words, he makes the greatest least. The first are made last.

The kingdom comes near, not far, again.

Even in Jerusalem, then, he has the last word. It makes of him a marked man. And even among this cultured crowd, the tension is palpable.

From now on, there will be no more sly talk of theology or law.

Only the conspiracies remain.

Quickly, then, Jesus and his circle have left the courtyard of the Gentiles, the farthest into the labyrinth of the temple a Gentile could go. They are standing in the courtyard of women, the farthest into the labyrinth of the temple a woman could go.

They sit in the courtyard, watching the swirl of people. Jesus is taking in as much of the life of the place as he can before the inevitable end comes. The disciples gawk at the fine robes of the rich. They parody the lift of their hands as they make their gift. The sound is heavy and deep in the metal basins, precious metals against metal.

Only Jesus takes in the poor widow amid the crowd.

She stands in the center of the yard. She is small and old and poor. Her thin hand emerges from beneath her cloak. Two little coins fall.

Only Jesus hears the tinny sound of the thin copper. Only Jesus takes the effort to hear.

Jesus turns and pulls the circle close once more. *Truly I tell you.*

By the whisper of his words, he makes the least greatest. The last first. The kingdom comes near, not far, once more.

When the disciples turn to look, they cannot find her. She has dissolved into the swirl of the crowd. Shortly they will leave the temple, never to return.

As I leave to walk in the warmth of day, my wife and our child go with me. They will go their own way when we reach the church. But when I turn toward the churchyard, our child demands to follow.

In the churchyard, he walks the labyrinth with me, while my wife reclines under a tree. I ask him if he wants to follow the path with me. I hold his hand. Then he lets go. He walks his own labyrinth, tiptoeing the bricks until he is distracted by something new, new to him. Then he returns. He arrives at the center with me. He walks on as I pray, nearly silently. He is moving in and out of the circle. He moves from margin and center to center and margin.

I hear him talk, in a child's plainsong rhythm: "This is a path. It goes around and around."

I delight in the miracle of his words.

I remember: *Whoever does not receive the kingdom of God as a little child will never enter it.* He is walking the labyrinth, its margin and center. He holds my hand. He is leading me through the labyrinth, from margin to center and center to margin. I walk it with him until I am distracted by something new, new to me.

My wife, his mother, watches us serenely until he asks to move on. My loves soon depart. I walk the path out of the labyrinth alone. The air is strangely quiet now that they are gone. A jet flies low overhead, a lonely hum in the wind. Under its tinny hum whispers the question.

I feel his whisper pulling me close. We stand eye to eye.

Truly I tell you . . . she out of her poverty has put in everything.

What is my poverty?

Out of what poverty can I give? Out of what can I give everything, all I have? Every life contains both its wealth and its poverty. Giving something out of my wealth is easy. Giving everything out of my poverty is hard. But this is how the least is made great. One requires only the authority of a credential. The other requires the authority of the person, whole and entire.

I walk the path of these thoughts. They go around and around.

36

To the West

ALL THIS BACK AND FORTH AGAIN: we wake to the sound of a storm. The drumbeat. The boom. The tick tock of hail. My son wakes up to it and calls for his mother. We wake up to a darkness deeper than midnight.

But the storm soon passes. And the shadow of darkness cannot hold back the light of day. The world is again calm for a moment.

I walk the labyrinth in a morning light saturated and shrouded by clouds. The ground is waterlogged. I have to step lightly. I am wary not to step in mud along the way. After the storm comes the song: a bird sings unseen. After the storm comes the song: a fire siren echoes unseen.

All these things foreseen but imminent. The signs point to the future storm night will bring, more fierce. Or so I am told.

All these things foreseen but imminent. There is an eschatology—an end game—to a labyrinth. There is a labyrinth in eschatology, the end of things. The way they turn over and over, already here, not yet there, already there, not yet here. Past and future meet on a path pushing to the end.

And at the end: past and future pull back from where things began. All things turning over and over in time. To walk their path is to enter a new time, a new way of keeping time, fast and slow, both at once.

卐

They step forward to turn back again (Mk 13:1-13 NIV). Beyond the heavy door, down the stone steps, they turn back to look from whence they came. As they move, they squint in the strobing sunlight. They walk in the stripes of shadow and light, a cityscape jungle. The voids between buildings open up ever-turning perspectives. *What massive stones! What magnificent buildings!* They gape at the skyscrapers of the city, tourists amid towers. They stare up as they walk in the trance of the city.

As gawking tourists always seem to do, they collide into the person in front of them, who is standing still. He does not look up. His eye is parallel with the ground, looking into their eyes. *Do you see all these great buildings?* They glance again at the stone and the glass and the steeples of iron.

The city towers around them. The city swirls around them.

Every one will be thrown down.

The disciples follow him out of the city. Time speeds, then slows, as they stand at the edge of the city of cities.

After a long silence: *Tell us, when will this be?* (NRSV).

They now sit on the hill opposite the city, facing the west. The temple stands before them, scraping the sky. As the end draws near, Jesus turns to the end, to death and the future. The beginning of the end turns to the end of the end. The end game. *What will be the sign?* Behind the temple, the clouds menace the horizon, the storm night will bring.

Jesus reads the signs in the storm.

Many will come in my name. Deception contains within it the seed of the end. *Wars and rumors of wars.* Violence contains within it the seed of the end. *Nation will rise against nation.* Discord contains within it the seed of the end. *Earthquakes . . . famines.* Destruction contains within it the seed of the end.

This is but the beginning of the birth pangs. This is how it has been. This is how it ever shall be. The beginning to the end to the beginning again. In death, the rebirth of life.

As for yourselves, beware. Suffering too contains within it the seed of the end.

But say whatever is given you at that time. The Spirit speaks in the seed of the end. In the midst of deception and violence, discord and destruction, suffering and hatred and betrayal, the good news of the kingdom is the seed of the end. It breaks open and breaks forth a new beginning in the end. It is the rebirth of life in death.

Jesus speaks with his eye focused in the distance, to the west. A thunderhead storms the horizon. Behind it, in the unseen distance, is light that will not be held back.

Past and future meet on a path pushing to the end.

This is why most labyrinths open and offer exit in the west. They begin and end in the west. Their path is a map of what is already and not yet.

At the exit to the labyrinth, I am looking to the west, to the future of this day, shrouded by clouds. I search the sky for signs.

The west: the direction of the setting sun, the direction of death. One enters and exits the labyrinth toward death.

The west: the direction of the future, the direction of hope. One enters and exits the labyrinth toward the future of life. To walk the labyrinth is to begin and end in the direction of death, at the same time to end and begin in the future of life.

This is the eschatology of the labyrinth, an end game.

Perhaps this is also why the labyrinth is drawn in the shape of a seed, a grain of wheat. It contains within it its end as a seed, its center, the end in the beginning. The beginning in the end. The tulips with their short-lived bloom. The squirrel entombed in a trash can. All things contain within them the seed of the end. All seeds contain within them both beginning and end.

I look to the west, to the future of this day and its night, of every day after this day. I am finding what I didn't know to seek, what I could never have sought.

This is the eschatology of the labyrinth, an end game.

37

A Memory

I REMEMBER THE TASTE OF FRESH FIGS.

I don't know why, but I walk the labyrinth remembering the taste of fresh figs. The sun has broken through the fractured stones of cloud, remnants of the storm. But the wind has retained an icy chill. The sun is warm, but the wind is cold. They meet and mix on the surface of earth.

I walk the labyrinth and remember a summer of my youth. I spent a week in San Antonio. I was on a "servant event" with my high-school youth group, a week spent serving Latino children in a vacation Bible school. I remember the old couple who hosted me in their home. I remember when our picture was taken the last day I was there, the way they both took my hands in theirs, unexpectedly, a sign of affection. I remember how every morning, before the day rose hot, they would pick fresh figs from the tree in the front of their yard. The fruit would sit in a bowl on the kitchen table as I rose from bed.

I remember how the old couple laughed when I asked them if they tasted like Fig Newtons. They insisted I try them. I remember the cool taste of fresh figs. The crush of the skin. The plush red flesh. The lush texture. The honey-sweet taste. In the heat of midsummer, the figs were perfectly ripe.

I remember how astonished I was by the surprise of figs in summer.

It will be nearly forty years later when those who will remain from among the Twelve, from among their generation, will gather again to this holy place, when they will remember these words (Mk 13:24-37). Jerusalem will lie in ruins. The temple will lie in ruins. Its behemoth stones will sit in rubble. Empire will have risen up against this city in war and devastation.

They will have been gathered *from the four winds, from the ends of the earth to the ends of heaven.* The messengers will be gathered together.

And then they will remember these words, spoken on a hill outside the city. The way the look of his eyes takes on the look of a prophet, to look through the veil of history, to perceive the changing orders of the world, to see a vision transcending time. The way his words reverberate with the oracles of the prophets of old, oracles of exile and return. The way he rises to stand among them, as if he were already lifted up on this hill, his shadow darkening the earth.

And on this day, nearly forty years later, the Son of Man will have gathered them together again by his words. These things will have taken place, and it will feel as if the heaven and earth that they know now in this day, here on this hill, will have all passed away.

But his words will have endured. And the words will have gathered them together again.

As I was then, I am astonished now by the madeleine memory of the taste of fresh figs.

In the churchyard, the branches of the trees are tender. They sway lithely in the wind. All around me, the trees are clothed in new leaves. Despite the chill in the air, summer is near. The fruit of summer shall soon be sweet.

So I will keep watch for the surprises of summer.

If I imagine the circuits of the labyrinth as an ascent up and around a hill, I am hiking the slope to its top. At the center, I stand at the top. I stand to keep watch for the coming of summer and the Son of Man.

They come in the clouds with glory like the sun.

I pray to keep awake. *Thy kingdom come.*

I pray to keep watch. *Thy will be done on earth as it is in heaven.*

Is this the day? Is this the hour? From the four winds, where the warmth meets the chill, the word of the Son of Man gathers again.

卐

Walking the Mount of Olives, Jesus has finally found a tree bearing fruit. On the top of this hill—out of season—a fig tree has grown ripe figs. The disciples are astonished by the surprise of summer figs in springtime.

A few of them have noticed men working in the distance of the valley. Gardeners are chopping down another fig tree, withered and dead.

The corner of his lip glistens as he talks. His watering mouth smacks as he speaks. Jesus is savoring the fruit he loves best. The sweet air mixing in the trees, rustling young leaves, hints of summer. The figs he plucks, their honey-sweet taste, inspire parables.

But about that day or hour no one knows.

The surprise of figs inspires stories to keep them awake.

卐

Like a ripe fig in springtime. Like a man on a journey. Like the stewards he leaves behind. Keep alert. Keep awake. Keep watch. Evening, midnight, cockcrow or dawn, the Son of Man will suddenly return.

Like the surprise of a memory seemingly forgotten. Like the madeleine memory of a summer fig in springtime.

I ascend the labyrinth awake and alert, to keep watch.

For what exactly? It will be hard to say. Jesus does not say. But the life of God has come near, in compassion and truth. Already here, not yet there.

I am awakened to its coming. I seek to find where it is already here. I seek to find where it is not yet there. Always a surprise. In these last few days, I stay awake for its coming. To keep awake for its coming here in this day, now in this hour, I ascend the hill, to watch and to pray.

For the kingdom has already come, and will yet come again.
It is the will done on earth the same as in eternity.
It is the future that comes now as a memory.
I pray to keep watch for its coming.

38

Anonymous

I WAIT UNTIL THE LATE AFTERNOON TO WALK. I wait until the cold of morning has dissipated to a cool, crisp late day. The clouds dissolve into the sky, light blue. The wind is gentle. Lawnmowers purr the neighborhood.

A rabbit, a robin and a squirrel—the labyrinth's anonymous residents—bound away from me as I enter the churchyard through its narrow passage. They make way for their frequent guest.

I walk the labyrinth to contemplate another memory, a beautiful anonymity.

She had been following them (Mk 14:1-11 NIV). Ever since the Mount of Olives, when she hid behind a tree to listen to the Son of Man speak, she had been following them. She followed them down the other slope, away from Jerusalem, to a house in Bethany. She followed at a distance into nightfall.

She stands now at the threshold of the house.

She holds in her hands all she has brought with her. She had bought it as a preparation for Passover, a costly extravagance. Had she known whom she would meet along the way, she would have brought something else, something different, something more. Or would she? She doesn't know. What shall she do? She hears the sounds of the meal inside. She is uninvited. She hears the warmth of conversation. She hears the sound of his voice. All that is within her wishes to respond to the beckon of his voice. She hears it like a whisper under the babbling water of noise, an invitation.

So she acts.

Swiftly she enters the room. The room falls silent. Her nervous fingers fumble on the neck of the clay jar, until in her haste she breaks it off. The fragrance of Indian blossoms fills the room. She stands behind the Son of Man sitting at the table and lifts the jar in her hands, above her head.

She begins to pour.

It splashes his scalp, runs down his head, in streams down his cheeks, douses the stubble of his jaw. He crooks his head upward and closes his eyes, receiving her benediction, grace to grace. The nard runs over his shoulder, drizzles his chest, seeps into his tunic.

The broken jar is now empty above him.

The silence of the room evaporates. The antagonism rises with a mannish bravado, like heat. They rise above her. *Why this waste?* The sound of the scolding is shrill, but she does not cower. She stands defiant before them. She has acted as love has required, in costly extravagance, and she will not be ashamed. She does what she did in the costly extravagance of love.

Jesus rises.

His incensed aura overwhelms the air. He rebukes the rebuke. *She has done a beautiful thing. The poor you will always have with you.*

But you will not always have me.

Here lies the irony of poverty, so often misinterpreted. To act in condescending charity is to keep the last last. To act in the costly extravagance of love makes the last first. This is the beautiful thing. In anointing the Son of Man, she anoints the poor into the extravagant impulses of love. She makes the last first. She anoints them into the extravagant mystery of God. This is the beautiful thing. And it is his disciples' last lesson in the mystery of the reign of God.

Because, in doing what she did, she anoints his body for death.

His body, drenched with beauty, is now embalmed for death.

卐

I walk the labyrinth to contemplate the anonymous act of an anonymous woman to be remembered forever. We shall never know her name. We know her by the beauty of her act, its beautiful anonymity. I sing her memory.

Were you there when she christened him for death?
Were you there when she christened him for death?
Oh . . . sometimes it causes me to tremble, tremble, tremble.
Were you there when she christened him for death?

The world is filled with innumerable pretty things, lovely things. But the beautiful things—the truly beautiful—happen when an act corresponds to an occasion in stunning convergence. It is the poignancy of the moment, where meaning meets memory, the holy accidents of existence. The beauty is in the synchronicity of it, its synergy. It makes of the act and the occasion an *event*. The beauty is in the event.

The way a toast makes friends of guests.

The way a random song over the air embodies the mood of a day.

The way two minds can meet on a subway train, the delight of their conversation.

The way an image arrests the eye for reasons we can't quite explain.

These are the ebenezers of our existence. We mark them when we can, the way Jacob marked the ground with stone at the site of a dream.

But many go nameless but for our memory of them, jars broken open by the hand of love.

The labyrinth is an ebenezer. It marks a site where meaning meets memory. Its artistry is ancient and anonymous. Its canvas bears no signature, the anonymous act of an anonymous person.

The labyrinth bears a beautiful anonymity.

As such, it defies any notion of the individual artist, a solitary genius making it famous from within. Rather, the labyrinth invites a common participation from outside of itself. The labyrinth bears forth the artistry of community. In walking its path, we walk the path of a thousand generations. We walk their anonymous beauty. A thousand generations have given shape and meaning to the curves of its design.

The labyrinth is a jar broken open by the hands of love.

We are its anonymous artists. To walk the labyrinth is to be gathered into a collective artistry, to be a fellow artist in its sublime art, a costly extravagance.

This is the beautiful thing.

And these beautiful things cannot be plotted nor planned. The plotting betrays the beauty. They happen. They simply happen. They are a spontaneous combustion of time and space in the impulse of a moment. The beauty is the synchronicity of it.

Beauty is synchronicity.

Every time it happens, we are remembering the story of the woman with a jar of pure nard. The event is its good news. Every time it happens, she is remembered. Hers is the beautiful anonymity of holy accidents, the meeting of act and occasion in stunning synchronicity. These things form the center of the labyrinth of life. We twist and turn around them until they happen again.

When they happen, they make the place sacred, an ebenezer, hallowed ground.

She has anointed my body beforehand for its burial (NRSV).

Nobody knows it now, but the fragrant oil is a chrism. This is the singular occasion, the cause for extravagance. That which the disciples hoped was still far off has now come near. On the eve of Passover, the time for ransom has now come. Its exotic incense fills the air.

He who was *one of the Twelve* stands now at the threshold. Had he known what he was about to do he never would have come. He would have gone somewhere else, somewhere different. What shall he do? He hears the sound of the meal resume. He has returned the invitation. He hears the warmth of conversation return. He will not take part. He hears the sound of his voice, a whisper under the babbling water of noises. And all that is within him is divided by the beckoning of his voice.

So he acts.

In a Gospel of paradoxes, we come now to the paradox of the traitor disciple. One of the inner circle will break the circle. The paradox of death will be set into motion by the paradox of betrayal. He has a name. His name is Judas. In Mark's telling of the story, we are told little more about him. His name is all we need to know. He is the paradox that sets into the motion the paradox of the end. He stands before the chief priests, a paradox. But he provides a solution to their dilemma. The deadly plot lurches forward, and the mystery of the kingdom becomes a murder mystery. The end game grows treacherous.

I sing his memory too.

Were you there when they plotted how he'd die?
Were you there when they plotted how he'd die?
Oh . . . sometimes it causes me to tremble, tremble, tremble.
Were you there when they plotted how he'd die?

Yet in the midst of paradox stands beauty. In the impending of death is beauty. The words echo in Judas' ear as he walks away:

Wherever the good news is proclaimed in the whole world, what she has done will be told.

At the center of the labyrinth I meet her, fellow pilgrim, anonymous. She holds in her hands an empty jar. It contains good news. She has found what she never could have sought. She has found what I never sought.

I seek what she found by singing her story.

Good news is proclaimed again in the singing of the story. It is her story. I am telling her story. This is the beautiful thing.

39

Silence

IT RAINED AGAIN IN THE NIGHT. And in the midmorning the skies darkened to charcoal and the clouds broke open in a downpour. The rain has now cleared. But the overcast sky still threatens more rain.

I arrive at the labyrinth under a heavy sky. I feel the weight of sad time.

The afternoon is calm, mild, humid. But the rain makes the air feel clean. The rain makes the world feel transparent and empty. How can a world so heavy laden feel so empty?

Today is Friday. I am in the middle day of the Triduum, the Three Days.

Good Friday.

Sad time.

Tonight I will celebrate the Tenebrae, the service of shadows, the extinguishing of lights. Last night, I remembered the meal before death.

I remember a childhood of Good Fridays. I remember how it always seemed that Good Fridays were destined for clouds and for rain. God was sad. It always seemed to darken to rain on Good Friday. And we would sing strange, haunting songs of the end. A death march.

Or so I remember of my childhood of Good Fridays.

The Gospel doesn't tell us how, but somehow Jesus has prepared beforehand a place for them (Mk 14:12-26). He has prepared a meal to remember. A meal for remembering. The meal to remember the decisive acts of God to save. The exodus. Liberation from slavery.

A new beginning near the end.

The two disciples know he has prepared a place beforehand because of the sign he has prepared. All the other water jars are carried by women. He told them to look for the man who carries a jar of water.

When they arrive, the Twelve are awestruck by the costly extravagance of the room, the *large room upstairs.* The woven cushions for sitting. The widespread rug of wool. The low-slung table of olive wood. The plastered walls dance in the flickering flames of lamps and candles. The disciples, born dirt poor, will have never had experienced the costly extravagance of such a room. The room is prepared by the hands of love.

But the table set before them is stark.

It is the Passover meal, a meal made for haste and for travel.

Jesus takes his place at the head of the table.

One of you will betray me. In the midst of extravagance, he begins the meal by foreshadowing the treachery to follow it. The room brims with the anguish of it. *Surely not I?* But the betrayer is not singled out. To the disciples, who it is remains a mystery within the mystery. They will eat together—they will be made a family together—in a room fraught with treachery.

He says the blessing:

Blessed are you, Lord our God, king of the world,
who brings forth bread from the earth.

They are each transported back to childhood, to memories of this night, father blessing the meal, the family sharing a table. But his further blessing of the meal—of the mystery that lies hidden under its bread and wine—defies their childhood memories.

He lifts the broken bread. *This is my body.*

He lifts the brimming cup. *This is my blood of the covenant, which is poured out for many.*

The words are stripped and stark, a graveyard of words. As the circle eats and drinks, they wince, anticipating the gore of a final miracle. But the bread tastes of wheat. And the cup tastes of fruit from the vine. The stark paradox of a hidden meal. Unaware, they partake of his death. And in their heart of hearts they feel a twinge, the beginning of a yearning for a new feast.

This is a meal for remembering.

The memory is love.

I approach the churchyard in silence, amid silences. The café is open, but the patio is empty. The street is nearly empty. Someone has cut down the bare tulip stalks along the wall. The rain forced the dogwood trees to drop most of their petals. Their fleshy wafers strew the grass. All along the way, robins hop the ground. I suspect they are looking for earthworms breaking the surface of a waterlogged earth. Two robins skip the churchyard as I walk the labyrinth.

Even the robins are silent.

When they had sung the hymn. According to the ritual of the Passover, they would have sung the Egyptian Hallel, Psalms 113–18.

When Israel went out from Egypt,
  the house of Jacob from a people of strange language,
Judah became God's sanctuary,
  Israel his dominion. . . .
Tremble, O earth, at the presence of the LORD,
  at the presence of the God of Jacob,
who turns the rock into a pool of water,
  the flint into a spring of water. (Ps 114)

The sound of their singing sounds strangely haunting, emptied by the sense of the end. This hymn of freedom is made this night into a death march.

I walk the labyrinth, singing a song made strange, the only sound amid silence.

Were you there when he broke the bread for them?
Were you there when he broke the bread for them?
Oh . . . sometimes it causes me to tremble, tremble, tremble.
Were you there when he broke the bread for them?

Were you there when they shared the cup of death?
Were you there when they shared the cup of death?
Oh . . . sometimes it causes me to tremble, tremble, tremble.
Were you there when they shared the cup of death?

I sing my way to the center. I shut tight my eyes to pray. I pray the Lord's Prayer in slow, halted breaths at the center of the labyrinth. I breathe in through my nose, then exhale each broken fragment of a petition, each petition its own breath.

Our Father
who art
in heaven
hallowed be
thy name
thy kingdom
come
thy will be
done
on earth
as it is
in heaven
give us
this day
our daily bread
forgive us
our trespasses
as we forgive
those

who trespass
against us
lead us not
into temptation
deliver us
from evil
for thine is
the kingdom
the power
the glory
forever
and ever
Amen

I pray it strangely, in a staccato whisper. As I open my eyes, I squint at the newfound brightness of light. I spot a butterfly with dark wings darting in the churchyard. It perches in the dogwoods. I watch it flutter high and low before it glides over the slate roof of the sanctuary, out of sight. To me, this day, it is the sign of the rebirth in death, gliding out of sight.

I begin to exit the labyrinth. A robin flies across my path to light on the head of the wooden man with a wooden ladder. The robin stands watch as I walk. As I make my way down the slope, away from the churchyard, I turn to take one last look back.

The robin is gone.

The close circle of disciples departs for the Mount of Olives. The hint of treachery still hangs heavy but empty in the air. They walk in a syncopated downbeat, an asymmetrical circle. The sounds of the night intone in minor keys.

They enter the garden as one. But they will leave it in a run, disbanded, dejected. Each will leave it in a different direction—deserters—lost, confused, defeated. Scattered to exile, they will leave him bare and alone.

From here, he will be handed over to condemnation, rejection, suffering.

They will each betray him in their own way, treacherous acts. And in the center of their hearts, they will feel themselves slaves again to the fear that rises within them.

Little did they know when they first followed this man that this was what they would find. Little did they know what they were seeking. They couldn't have known what they would find.

What they find is suffering unto death. They feel its sting in their fear.

As I walk away, I sing into the silence a song made strange.

Were you there when we fearful fled away?
Were you there when we fearful fled away?
Oh . . . sometimes it causes me to tremble, tremble, tremble.
Were you there when we fearful fled away?

40

Exit

It is raining. It has been raining all day. So, in midmorning, I walk with an umbrella, a black umbrella. Strange: now at the end, despite all the tortuous transformations of the seasons, this is the first day I have to physically walk in the rain. On the way, I stop to buy a newspaper.

Last night brought tornadoes to the city. The destruction made national news. The sirens—twice—interrupted our Tenebrae. We finished the liturgy outside the sanctuary, in the downstairs dining hall, our own upper room. And it felt as if friends were made into family. We concluded with the loud noise of the *strepitus*—a book was slammed shut—and the last candle was walked out of the room.

We ended in song.

Were you there when they laid him in the tomb?
Were you there when they laid him in the tomb?
Oh . . . sometimes it causes me to tremble, tremble, tremble.
Were you there when they laid him in the tomb?

I walk the way to the labyrinth in the rain, under an umbrella. Strange: how the canopy of an umbrella focuses me to a point. I walk under a low canopy of shadows. I walk in darkness to keep myself dry. I cannot see the sky nor the tops of the trees. I cannot look for birds. All I can hear is the tic-tic-tic-tic of raindrops slapping the stretched nylon, a timer ticking to the inevitable end of time.

Occasionally I shake the umbrella and the lines of water fall around me, lines that make a cylinder of water encircling me, a halo of rain. Underneath the umbrella's skin, its metal spines make its own kind of labyrinth. All the lines lead to the same center above my head.

My eyes are focused on the way before me, the steps right before me, and to the center toward which they lead, an inevitable end.

Along the way, the sidewalk along the street squirms with long, stretched-out worms escaping death by drowning. I walk too quickly to know whether they escape the death of my foot. In places I leap over puddles. In places I walk along the curb to avoid long pools of water.

Along the way, I tuck the newspaper under my arm to keep it dry.

I approach the labyrinth from the west. From death. From the future. All its news is tucked under my arm.

As I draw near the labyrinth, I smell the musty odor of incense, from I don't know where, I don't know how.

It reminds me, if I needed reminding.

I am approaching a sacred place, an ebenezer, holy ground.

Silence and noise. All that now surrounds Jesus of Nazareth is a reverberating back and forth between silence and noise (Mk 15:1-47). He is surrounded by noise. But he is silent. He stands silent before the noise of a justice subverted.

We heard him say (Mk 14:58). The noise that swirls around him is all hearsay. Irony amid irony, the charges against a man who refuses to speak are against, of all things, what the man *said.* Yet the testimonies cannot agree. And now he says nothing. The hero of the story, the man whose life was action and authority and power, now stands the silent victim. The story made tragic and strange, the tragic hero stands amid silence and noise.

The plot of the tragic was already inevitably clear. *Betray. Condemn. Hand over. Mock. Spit upon. Flog. Kill.* The Son of Man had already made its tragic end clear. Now he reaches the end.

The end is death.

Death is always the end of tragedy.

But only here is the revelation made clear. It comes in the horrifying noise of the crowd.

Crucify him.

Never before in this telling of the story has the method of his death been made clear.

In Mark's Gospel, the only crosses mentioned up to this very moment are the crosses taken up by Jesus' followers to bear after him. Never before has the cross been *his* to bear.

Walking the circling way up the hill, he bears now a cross that takes up the pain and suffering and death of all who have followed in his path. He bears up the pain of the world, broken and fractured and bleeding. And only Simon of Cyrene can have an inkling of its burden, the splinters of wood drawing a trickle of blood from his flesh.

This cross is his alone to bear.

He hangs from it as bitter fruit from a tree, wrapped in thorns.

Only then does he speak, and what he speaks is stripped bare by torture and pain. His words are the noise of the betrayed, the condemned, the dying.

Eloi, Eloi, lema sabachthani?

The words are so haunting the Gospel leaves them in the language the Galilean himself spoke, too excruciating to translate into a common tongue.

My God, my God, why have you forsaken me? The question is simultaneously a plea and an accusation. Jesus prays the paradoxical prayer of the psalm, a song made strange. His face is bruised black and blue, mottled with tortuous streaks of blood.

His body hangs on the verge of death.

He hangs there as the paradox to end all paradoxes, the mystery at the end of mystery.

The One sent by God, forsaken by God.

The tragic hero dying the death of the common criminal. Above his head reads his title: *King*. And only in the midst of a tragic paradox can the jest be made true.

What comes next becomes the end of silence and the end of noise. In the midst of noise, there is one final cry. Jesus shrieks a deafening cry.

It is his last breath.

The rabbi, the prophet, the Christ, is dead.

The Gospel's former swift movement—its immediacy—swiftly returns. The body now lies in a tomb, in the earth, behind the pitch-black shadow of rock. And immediately, even in death, the Son of Man draws people from the four winds around him. Simon of Cyrene. The centurion from Rome. Joseph of Arimathea. The women from Galilee. North, south, east and west. They are gathering from the four winds to lay the Son of Man to rest.

This is the end of the tragedy.

Exit. Death march.

The remaining actors walk off the stage. The tragic drama is at its end. The noise of death is done.

All the earth falls silent.

I walk the labyrinth with my eyes focused on the steps before me, the ground itself. Slick grass. Slippery brick. The ground sloshes under my footfalls. My eyes are focused to the point on the path before each step, so focused that I reach the center more quickly than I thought I would, a surprise. Under the shadow of the umbrella, my sight so limited, the center isn't as much a center of a circle as it is simply the end of a path. I lift the umbrella, and with it my eyes, to see again the maze as a whole.

Strange. Only now, this day in the rain, do I see it.

The only straight lines in the path, the short dashes of lines that force the pilgrim to stop and turn, occur along the axes of the four winds—like a compass—north, south, east, west. Only now, with my vision focused to a point by the canopy of shadow, do I see that I stand at the center of a cruciform path. The dotted straight lines—north, south, east and west—embed a hidden cross amid tortuous circles.

Only now do I see it. This labyrinth has taken the cross that is the first step to draw the Cretan maze and hidden it in its center.

How could I have missed it for so long?

Strange: to find what I never sought, to find what had been long hidden, a cross hidden in earth.

The cross is the sign hidden in the shape of a labyrinthine earth, square in circle. The cross is the compass of earth. All these days, I have been walking the path of my cross. I stand at its center, its vortex. It bears the body of my Lord, the Christ. He is lifted up on my cross like bitter fruit from a tree.

Only now do I see him, face to face.

If the labyrinth is love, this is the Tree of Life at its center.

Standing in its center—its axis, its vortex—I see him, face to face.

I lift my eyes and catch the vision of a cross etched into stone, a small emblem on the sanctuary's north face. Again, I had not seen this other cross until today. I pray with my eyes fixed on it. The rain splashes my face. I blink in the face of the rain as I pray.

I make the sign of the cross four times, in each dotted-line direction, turning clockwise. South, east, north, west. I turn in a circle to make the sign of the cross to the four winds.

It is said that under the pavement of some of the cathedral labyrinths of Europe, under its center, the architect of the cathedral is buried. It is the architect's seal, his signature, on the structure. It is a crafty nod to Daedalus, the father of architects, the mythical inventor of the labyrinth. It makes of the labyrinth a tomb hewn out of rock.

Walking its path is walking into a tomb, the inevitable end.

Life is a labyrinth. At its center is death. The labyrinth marks the path to the tomb. Inside it, under ground, behind rock, lies the dead body of One called King of the Jews.

At the center is death: his death, my death.

Standing here, I wish. I wish. Part of me wishes I had never found what I didn't know I was seeking: my death, his death.

The other part of me is so glad, so grateful, to find what I have found at the end of this long-winding path: my death in his death.

I stand on the ground he has made holy by death.

I stand on the ground imprinted with his cross. South, east, north, west: the whole earth is imprinted with the sign of his cross, my cross.

I stand on this ground—the center of the earth—and find him, face to face.

part eight

After the End

For the first time, this last time, I rise up *very early on the first day of the week, just after sunrise* (Mk 16:2 NIV).

It is Sunday, the first day of a new week.

For the first time, this last time, I will walk the labyrinth on a Sunday. It is not raining, but the rain will come. Mist hangs in the air like lace. It is early morning and I am walking to the labyrinth.

Every step of the labyrinth has led to this place.

Every step has led to this day.

The forty-first day.

The first day of a new week.

After all the teaching and preaching, after all the miracles and power, after the walking on water and the sailing on the sea, after all the parables and secrets, after the suffering, the pain, the death, the women cannot bear not to see him (Mk 16:1-8 NIV). Their hearts are empty, broken jars hollowed out by the end. Everything they have known and unknown, everything they have sought and found, has been undone by the end.

Mary Magdalene, Mary and Salome cannot bear not to see him.

Even if he is lifeless and dead.

They walk a slow, circling path in the early morning. They walk in whispers. They walk in the quietness before waking. No one else, it seems, in the wide world has yet risen from slumber.

The slow sun is barely rising, a glowing sliver on the eastern horizon.

The women carry in their hands clay jars of fragrant spice. They come to anoint their dead King, costly extravagance, labor of love.

They remember the horrifying colors of his body, the colors of beating and scorn. They remember the blood. They remember the cry. They remember the stone.

They remember the stone. It will soon block their path to his body, into the tomb.

They whisper to each other the problem of death. *Who will roll the stone away?*

They slow to a stop. Arriving at the place, they now stand where the stone should be.

There is no stone.

As they look inside, their empty hearts are mirrored by an empty tomb, a broken jar hollowed out by a new beginning. The jars fall from their shocked hands, crashing to shards at their feet. Earthy sweetness wets their feet and overwhelms the air.

The young man, his tunic of white, sits before them. They barely hear his words. They barely hear him announce the miracle of this emptiness, the miracle of life from death. They barely hear him for the shock of terror that stands on the sheer edge of unknown, unsought joy.

Except for one word that rings clear. *Galilee.* They run trembling and mute from an empty tomb. They do not speak, but the words echo in their ears.

He is going ahead of you into Galilee.

Most ancient manuscripts that articulate the math of the *computus*—the lunar math used to calculate the annual date of Easter—draw the labyrinth as its symbol, sign of the journey from the Ash Wednesday of repentance to the Sunday of new life.

So, of all the things the labyrinth is, it is also—and finally—a calendar.

Every day I walked the labyrinth I was walking the calendar of days to this day.

The first day of a new week.

Every day I walked the labyrinth I was one day closer to this day.

This last day is the first day. Its calendar was calculated from the last day to the first day, from the end to find the beginning.

This first day of this new week is also called the eighth day. It is the day after the seven days of creation, the first day of a new beginning. It finds its symbol in the eight-sided baptismal font, the labyrinth of water, the first act of a new beginning in God.

I stand at the entrance to the labyrinth in the mist of early morning. The dew of the grass wets my feet.

No stone blocks my path.

The *computus* of resurrection lies before me.

I take the first step toward the last step of this last day, the first day of a new week.

The eighth day.

Outside the garden, the women stop their running to catch their breath. The women—Mary Magdalene, Mary and Salome—look into each other's faces. And from somewhere within, they know not where, courage rises. Huddled under a fig tree, leafy and green, they speak courage to each other. The light of morning begins to fill the earth. The terror of night turns to an edgy mist of hope. Courage wells up their hearts, broken jars brimming with its sweetness.

They must run to Galilee.

If the labyrinth is the womb of life, their lives are the womb in which faith in the Son of Man will first rise reborn, the firstfruit of those who rise.

But first, they must tell the others. They must give the news given to them. As night ends into day, this news becomes the beginning of good news.

This is the beginning of the good news.

They scatter to the four winds to find the others, darting down tortuous paths to find the disciples. The calling of their names sounds through the air. They find the disciples—one by one, scattered, tattered, alone. They find them—one by one—and speak the only words they remember.

He is going ahead of you into Galilee.

They speak it as a whisper into each disciple's ear, into Peter's ear. As they seek to find each hiding disciple, they speak the words close to his ear. There will be no mistaking what he hears. Courage wells up and overflows each time they speak the words. Into John's ear. Into James's ear. Into Andrew's ear. All of them, they whisper the words into each ear.

He is risen. He is going ahead of you into Galilee.

At each whisper, each disciple darts off in a sprint. Out of the city they run.

They must run to Galilee.

They each know only one road out of Jerusalem. They know only one tortuous path back to the beginning. It is the same road they walked to get here, to the center of this city, to the center of their empty hearts.

Each one runs the road back to Galilee. As they run, they meet up with each other along the road. They are a circle again, disciples, siblings.

The women lead the way.

The good news of the women brings them together again, a mysterious reunion. They run the road together again.

They run. They run. They run.

Into evening—through the night—into the next dawn. They run. They will not stop running. They will not stop until they reach the villages on the outskirts of Galilee.

They run with fear on their heels and hope in their eyes.

They run with the abandon of children, little ones, breathless and sweating.

They run with their hearts filled to bursting inside them, full from the speeding of their pulse, from the love that swells their blood.

In the distance, against the blue-orange horizon gilded with rising light, they see a solitary figure, running. They are chasing him. His minuscule silhouette grows a little larger with every step.

He is risen. He is going ahead. They are chasing after.

With each step, they are gaining ground to meet him.

There are medieval accounts of the cathedrals of Auxerre and Sens, in France, that describe the labyrinth dance of Easter. The chapter members of the cathedral monastery would gather along the outer circle, early in the morning. At the signal of dawn, they would begin to step a three-step dance around the edge of the labyrinth. And the dean of the monastery would step his own dance to walk the path, singing the Easter sequence of psalms and sacred songs.

In his hands he held a ball, a sphere large enough that it had to be held in both hands. He would throw the ball to the monks in the outer circle as he walked the path. And they would throw it back to him.

The Easter dance was also, then, a game. The monks were playing catch, a child's game. They were playing the unknown, unsought joy of Easter in a game children play.

I stand at the entrance to the labyrinth.

Everything is quiet, in the early morning before waking. Winslow's Home is dark, closed and quiet. The church is closed and quiet. Perhaps the pastor stirs inside, preparing for this holy day in the moments before waking. But I do not hear him.

I stand in the quiet of morning at the entrance to the labyrinth.

In my hands I carry a little red plastic ball, the size of a tennis ball.

I take the first step into the path. I toss the ball in the air as a game, the same game I played with a baseball as a child.

As I enter the labyrinth, I spontaneously step into a sequence. Not a dance really, just a stepping in rhythm. Every three steps I rock back and forth on my heels to then step forward again. But there is no pattern to it. I step as the spirit of the path moves me. I hold in my hands the red sphere, tossing it from one hand to the other.

I juggle the unknown, unsought joy of Easter.

How time flies in a game children play. I reach the center in what feels like seconds. I stop at the center. And as I've done every day of the calendar of this journey, I pray. I pray my daily prayer with both hands lifted up and out in the gesture of *orans*, the uplifted, outstretched gesture of prayers large enough to be held in both hands, lifted to God.

Then, on this eighth day, in the center of this labyrinth, for the first time this last time, I play. I toss the ball into the air as high as I can. As I did with a baseball when I was a child. Above the ball hanging in midair, I see sparrows gliding high. Above the sparrows, a jet flies. I hear a hoot in the trees. Perhaps an owl, perhaps a whippoorwill, I cannot tell.

This first time, this last time, the center of this labyrinth, on this eighth day, is an empty tomb. The twists and turns to the center are the path to the empty tomb. It is the Easter dance to the empty tomb of the Son of Man.

The center of the labyrinth is a jar broken open by a new beginning.

This is the beginning of the good news.

And now to think: after all the knowing and the not knowing, after the seeking and the finding, I seek and find again.

And again, the surprise.

An empty tomb. His tomb, my tomb: empty.

Christ resurrected resurrects me.

Standing in the center, I see Christ—the living Christ—face to face.

This is the beginning of the good news.

Standing at the empty tomb—his empty tomb, my empty tomb—I enter the kingdom of God as a little one, playing a child's game.

On the little red plastic ball I have written the words for this first day of a new week, this eighth day. I have written them in plain block letters with a black marker.

CHRIST IS RISEN! HALLELUJAH!

The words span the equator of the little globe in a circle, the beginning of good news to span the wide circle of the world.

There, at the empty tomb, the center of the labyrinth, I lay the ball in a tuft of thick green-growing grass. Today is Easter, the eighth day. I leave the ball as a gift—anonymous—for the next anonymous pilgrim who will walk this way. It is the gift of good news. It begins here, at the end.

And taking the first step from the center, I look to find Christ—the living Christ—face to face once again.

Christ, in the last.

Christ, in the least.

Christ, in the little ones.

Christ, the Lord of creation. Christ, the Lord in creation.

I look for Christ, once dead, now resurrected.

I look for Christ in the labyrinth of life.

Standing from the center, I look. I look. I look.

I am looking for the resurrection of the dead.

Then, from the center of the labyrinth, for the first time this last time, I run the path in sprints. Like Mary Magdalene, Mary and Salome, I sprint from the tomb. I stop and dart through the turns as in a high-school basketball drill. The twists and turns away from the center, away from the empty tomb, mark the one road back to where the journey started, back to Galilee.

I run. I run. I run the path home. I arrive at the door of my home and bow, my hands on my knees, breathless and sweating.

I walk through the door. I sit down to write.

Breathless and sweating, I sit down to write the resurrection, as best as I know how, an unknown, unsought joy.

This is the beginning of the good news.

The good news is the beginning in the end, beginning again.

The reborn reign of God breaks new again into the world. Into Galilee. The beginning of the good news is to begin again at Galilee. Where it all started. Where it all starts again. But never like it was before. Jesus Christ—the Son of God—stands there, in the center of Galilee, to start new life again.

To restart me in new life: from death, my death, to life, his life.

He revives me in unknown, unsought joy.

He is going ahead of me into Galilee. Into my Galilee. This is my Galilee. I stand in its center. I depart from it in new life, a new beginning. Every exit from the center—back into the twisting path of the labyrinth of life—is a new beginning.

Into my Galilee.

I exit the labyrinth—this last day, this first day, the eighth day—in the exhilaration of unknown, unsought joy.

The whole day rises exalted before me. I run back to Galilee, back to the beginning, back to wherever it is he stands resurrected. I run after him, to exult in the new life he leaves in his wake. I run after him, along the road others have run before me and yet others will run after me.

We meet up with each other along the way. We run together.

This day—and every day yet to come—I chase after the risen Christ. I look for the resurrection of the dead.

He is risen. He is going ahead. I am chasing after.

With each step, we are gaining ground to meet him.

Acknowledgments

CONTRARY TO POPULAR OPINION, writing is not a solitary process. The act of writing is often solitary, but writing itself is a social process, a collective process. Which means that every time a book is written, its writer is grateful to all the others who took part in the process, known and unknown.

I am deeply grateful. First and foremost, I owe a deep and abiding gratitude to my family, particularly to my spouse, Jennifer, and our two sons, Justin and Evan, not only for the sacrifices they made as I made this book but for the bottomless love, joy and energy they gave to make it a reality. Likewise, to my larger family, my parents, Jim and Marcy, and my brother, Josh.

Peter Mead has been an energizing creative force in my life for quite some time, and I am so grateful for it. At several important points in my career Dale Meyer has employed me in the service of words and the media that message them. A whole host of teachers and professors have nurtured a love for words in me that I will never outgrow, among them Barry Bobb, Rich Reiss, John Ruff, Gail McGrew Eifrig, Paul Contino, Ed Byrne, Tom Troeger, Lanny Hammer, Julija Sukys and Scott Cairns. As I was writing this book, numerous conversations with David Schmitt inspired me, whether or not he was aware. I wouldn't know what I know about the Gospel According to Mark without the superb commentary by R. T. France, but more importantly without several lengthy conversations with Jim Voelz, whose own commentary is now out. I first read

Jorge Luis Borges in a class taught by the late Richard Maxwell. But my enthusiasm for Borges was immeasurably deepened by hallway conversations with Jeff Kloha.

I owe thanks to Pastor Bill Perman and the people of First Presbyterian Church, for the generous hospitality of their congregation. Also to Dan Gill, who spent a particularly humid evening taking incredible photographs of First Presbyterian's labyrinth.

Finally, gratitude to a few people who made special contributions to this book. First, to Bob Fryling, Cindy Bunch and the staff at InterVarsity Press, who continually challenged me to make this book the book it needed to be. To John Nunes, who read several sections and shared wisdom to make it immeasurably greater, and whose close friendship is a deep and abiding benediction to me. And finally, to Walter Wangerin. I am humbled and honored that he chose to write the foreword to this book. The time I've spent in his presence and the innumerable words I've heard spoken from his mouth will bless me for the rest of my life.

All of these people, and more, made this book infinitely better. All its flaws remain my own.

Appendix

Ways to Walk a Labyrinth

In the United States, there are primarily two organizations that provide resources related to the labyrinth, the Labyrinth Society (http://labyrinthsociety.org) and Veriditas (http://veriditas.org). Together, they collaborate on a searchable online labyrinth locator (http://labyrinthlocator.com) to help anyone find a labyrinth in their local area or throughout the world.

Moreover, there are any number of firms and artisans, such as Labyrinth Enterprises LLC founded by labyrinth expert Robert Ferré, that design and construct labyrinths or rent out portable canvas labyrinths for events.

My Twitter feed (@travisjscholl) provides video podcasts of walks through various labyrinths, including the labyrinth I walked for forty days while writing this book, as a virtual experience of the labyrinth. A quick search on the Internet would reveal many, many more.

Churches or organizations can create their own labyrinths simply by making paths suitable for guided walking. For instance, one can draw a labyrinth pattern on a parking lot with chalk. Pews or chairs in a sanctuary can be used as dividers to create a back-and-forth path leading to a central focal point, like an altar or baptismal font. In a gymnasium, cones or masking tape can be used to chart a path leading to a central circle. All that is really needed to create the experience of walking a labyrinth is a defined, meandering path with a center or end point that allows for quiet contemplation and a way of exit.

The Labyrinth Society's website includes drawings of labyrinths that can be printed for personal use or as handouts, including a reproduction of the Chartres Cathedral labyrinth. Labyrinth drawings like these can be traced with a pen or pencil, or a finger, to reproduce the experience of walking the labyrinth.

Along these same lines, there are any number of miniature labyrinths, made of wood, stones or even potted plantings, that can be used to guide reflection by tracing the path with a finger or pointer. This would include labyrinthine games, like mazes where one guides pellets or balls through tunnels or rows by tilting the board up and down, back and forth.

Finally, one can imitate Daedalus and draw a seven-circuit Cretan labyrinth following instructions similar to the ones provided by Hermann Kern in his magisterial study *Through the Labyrinth* (34). Start by drawing a central cross, then draw a right angle within each quadrant formed by each arm of the cross. Place a dot inside the right angle of each quadrant. Then connect the dots and the ends of each line in an alternating pattern beginning with the upper arm of the cross and the vertical line of the right angle to its left, until all the arms and dots are connected (see the illustration). If you place two right angles within each arm of the cross, it will produce an eleven-circuit labyrinth. A little hint too: if you are going to then draw your way through the labyrinth, use a pen or pencil of a different color from the one you drew the labyrinth with. Otherwise, it can get a little confusing.

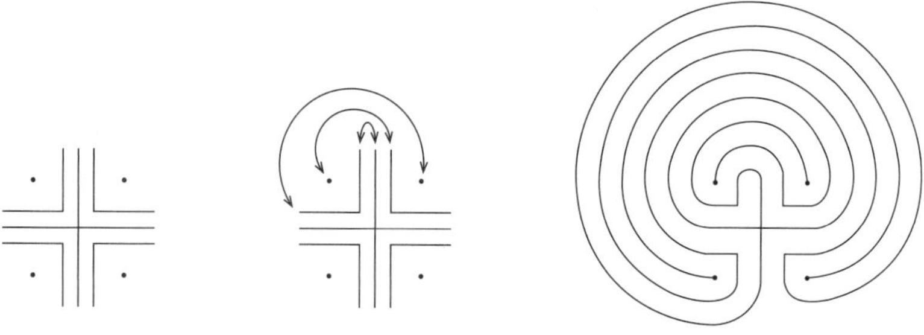

Figure 2

Notes

Part 1: Before the Beginning: Prologue

The epigraph from Jorge Luis Borges is taken from his short story "The Garden of Forking Paths," in *Labyrinths: Selected Stories and Other Writings*, ed. Donald A. Yates and James E. Irby (New York: New Directions, 1964), p. 23.

The loose paraphrase of Luther's thoughts about the right hand of God is a reference to his response to Ulrich Zwingli over their disagreements regarding the Eucharist at the Marburg Colloquy (1529).

Part 2: Christ, the Path

One of the more famous passages in Martin Luther's Large Catechism comes from his explanation of the First Commandment: "Anything on which your heart relies and depends, I say, that is really your God." See *The Book of Concord*, ed. Robert Kolb and Timothy Wengert (Minneapolis: Fortress, 2000), pp. 386-90.

"He is the one path that contains multitudes. He contains multitudes." These sentences are an allusion to Walt Whitman's "Song of Myself."

9: Rain

Martin Luther spoke of the *platzregen*, the passing rain shower, in several places, including his treatise "To the Councilors of all German cities, that they should establish and maintain Christian Schools" (1524), in *Luther's Works* (Minneapolis: Fortress, 1962), 45:352.

Part 3: The Way of Love

Robert Frost's poem referenced here and subsequently is "The Road Not Taken," in *The Poetry of Robert Frost: The Collected Poems, Complete and Unabridged*, ed. Edward Connery Lathem (New York: Henry Holt, 1979), p. 105.

Part 4: Calling, by Name

The phrase "A heap of broken images" comes from T. S. Eliot's poem "The Waste Land," in *Collected Poems, 1909-1962* (New York: Harcourt, Brace, 1963), p. 53.

The quotation by Luther that begins "Nothing is so small" is found in his "Confession concerning Christ's Supper" (1528), in *Martin Luther's Basic Theological Writings*, 2nd ed., ed. Timothy F. Lull (Minneapolis: Fortress, 2005), p. 272.

The "wise preacher" whom I paraphrase is the fictional John Ames in Marilynne Robinson's novel *Gilead* (New York: Farrar, Straus and Giroux, 2004), p. 210.

19: The Number Eleven

The phrase "living faith of the dead . . . dead faith of the living" echoes Jaroslav Pelikan's famous aphorism "Tradition is the living faith of the dead, traditionalism is the dead faith of the living," in *The Vindication of Tradition* (New Haven, CT: Yale University Press, 1986), p. 65.

20: Between the Lines

Annie Dillard writes about seeing and about the world being "planted in pennies" in *Pilgrim at Tinker Creek* (New York: Harper Perennial, 2007), pp. 16-17.

22: Cross

The lines from William Shakespeare's *King Lear* are the closing lines of the play (act 5, scene 3), in *The Pelican Shakespeare: King Lear* (New York: Penguin, 1970), p. 167.

Part 5: Practicing the Everyday

Jorge Luis Borges's story "The Gospel According to Mark" was first published in English in the *New Yorker*, October 23, 1971, pp. 40-42. It is also included in Borges's *Collected Fictions*, trans. Andrew Hurley (New York: Penguin, 1998), pp. 397-401.

25: Safe at Home

The line "The Child is father of the Man" comes from William Wordsworth's poem "My Heart Leaps Up When I Behold," in *Favorite Poems* (Mineola, NY: Dover, 1992), p. 34.

Part 6: The Things We Keep and Leave Behind

The Coldplay lyric is, literally, "Nobody said it was easy / No one ever said it would be this hard," from the song "The Scientist" on the album *A Rush of Blood to the Head* (Capitol, 2002).

The quotation from Frederick Buechner comes from *Wishful Thinking: A Seeker's ABC* (New York: HarperCollins, 1993), p. 118.

31: Running Late

The paragraph that begins, "I can feel time slow to a rhythm with half-lit radiance" alludes to passages in Norman Maclean's story "A River Runs Through It," in *"A River Runs Through It" and Other Stories* (Chicago: University of Chicago Press, 1976), pp. 103-4.

Part 7: The Way of the Cross

This popular quotation from Søren Kierkegaard exists in various forms. See *Papers and Journals: A Selection*, trans. Alastair Hannay (New York: Penguin, 1996), pp. 63, 161.

I transcribed the lines from the DVD of the film *Shadowlands*, directed by Richard Attenborough (1993; HBO Home Video, 1999). The film dramatizes the relationship between C. S. Lewis and Joy Davidman, their marriage, and her early death from cancer, which inspired Lewis's classic book *A Grief Observed*.

The line "The world is too much with us" is from William Wordsworth's poem "The World Is Too Much with Us; Late and Soon," in *Favorite Poems* (Mineola, NY: Dover, 1992), p. 53.

The quotation from Dietrich Bonhoeffer comes from *The Cost of Discipleship*, trans. R. H. Fuller (New York: Touchstone, 1995), p. 89.

Further Reading

On labyrinths in general, their history and in literature:

Borges, Jorge Luis. *Labyrinths: Selected Stories and Other Writings*. New York: New Directions, 2007.

Doob, Penelope Reed. *The Idea of the Labyrinth: From Classical Antiquity Through the Middle Ages*. Ithaca, NY: Cornell University Press, 1990.

Kern, Hermann. *Through the Labyrinth: Designs and Meanings over 5,000 Years*. English edition. New York: Prestel, 2000.

Matthews, W. H. *Mazes and Labyrinths: Their History and Development*. New York: Dover, 2011.

Wright, Craig. *The Maze and the Warrior: Symbols in Architecture, Theology, and Music*. Cambridge, MA: Harvard University Press, 2004.

On the Gospel According to Mark:

France, R. T. *The Gospel of Mark*. New International Greek Testament Commentary. Grand Rapids: Eerdmans, 2002.

Rhoads, David, Joanna Dewey and Donald Michie. *Mark as Story: An Introduction to the Narrative of a Gospel*. 3rd edition. Minneapolis: Fortress, 2012.

Voelz, James. *Mark 1–8*. Concordia Commentary. St. Louis: Concordia Publishing House, 2013.

Daily Scripture Readings Index

Formatio books from InterVarsity Press follow the rich tradition of the church in the journey of spiritual formation. These books are not merely about being informed, but about being transformed by Christ and conformed to his image. Formatio stands in InterVarsity Press's evangelical publishing tradition by integrating God's Word with spiritual practice and by prompting readers to move from inward change to outward witness. InterVarsity Press uses the chambered nautilus for Formatio, a symbol of spiritual formation because of its continual spiral journey outward as it moves from its center. We believe that each of us is made with a deep desire to be in God's presence. Formatio books help us to fulfill our deepest desires and to become our true selves in light of God's grace.